Life Application Family Devotions

life
APPLICATION
Family Devotions

Len Woods

Tyndale House Publishers, Inc.
Wheaton, Illinois

Library of Congress Cataloging-in-Publication Data

Woods, Len.
  Life application family devotions / Len Woods.
    p. cm.
  Includes index.
  ISBN 0-8423-3750-4 (pbk. : alk. paper)
  1. Family—Prayer-books and devotions—English. 2. Family—Religious life.
3. Christian life. I. Title.
BV255.W67 1997
249—dc21   97-8873

Printed in the United States of America

01 00 99 98 97
7   6   5   4   3   2   1

To Mom, Dad, Jack, Jan, and Ellen—
my precious family members,
who taught and modeled
the truths contained in these pages

CONTENTS

INTRODUCTION

Most Christian parents want to have family devotions. They can imagine a cozy time of reading the Bible and praying together with their children. Unfortunately, most children couldn't care less. How can parents get their children interested and involved?

This book can help.

Life Application Family Devotions contains 150 entries that will help you get your children involved in family devotions and curious about what the Bible says. Each devotional begins with a provocative, real-life vignette designed to stimulate conversation about important life values. Read this part out loud to your children (or have an older child read it to the others). Then ask the questions in the "Talk about It" section. Feel free to ask further questions to get the discussion going deeper. Then look up and read the Bible passage listed in the "Check It Out" section, and read the note under "Apply It." Allow time to discuss this passage further. Each devotional also includes a "Tip for Parents" with advice for discussing the topic.

Discussion can be challenging when you have younger and older children together. We recommend starting with the youngest and moving to the oldest. Make sure you allow enough time for each child to answer. Don't let the older children criticize the answers of the younger ones. Remember that getting off track in your discussion may lead to a topic your family needs to discuss.

Select a regular time for your family to enjoy these devotionals. We recommend right after dinner, but you could also discuss them at the breakfast table or later in the evening. Choose a time that is the most conducive to conversation in your family.

Author's Note: The vignettes in this book are based on the actual dilemmas of real people. However, the names used in each scenario are not intended to ascribe certain behaviors to specific real-life individuals or families. Any resemblance between a character in this book and a real person is entirely coincidental.

Alcohol

Jamie is spending the night with her friend Rachel. After Rachel's parents go to bed, the girls sneak back downstairs.

"Where are we going?" Jamie whispers.

"Just follow me!" Rachel replies.

When the girls get downstairs, Rachel goes into the pantry and silently retrieves a bottle of bourbon.

"What's that?" Jamie asks, her eyes big with surprise.

"Some kind of whiskey or something. People who do business with my dad give it to him every year at Christmastime. We have about four bottles of it."

"I didn't know your parents drink."

"They don't. But I've seen my mom use this stuff on fruitcakes and other recipes. That's why I grabbed this particular bottle. It's already open!"

"So?"

"So we can taste it."

Jamie is suddenly nervous. "I don't know, Rachel. What if your parents catch us?"

"My parents could sleep through a train wreck!"

"Yeah, but what if your mom realizes some of it is gone?"

"Oh, as if! Jamie, we're not gonna drink the whole bottle. Let's just sip some of it and see what it's like."

Jamie is scared to death, but she also wants to be cool. "Um, OK, how do we do it?"

"Your guess is as good as mine. I guess just swig it."

Jamie goes first. No sooner does the whiskey touch her tongue than she spits it into the sink. "Yecchhhh!" she hisses. "That's terrible."

"I've heard that people mix it with soft drinks and orange juice," Rachel suggests.

"Anything would be better than drinking it plain," Jamie says with a nod.

Just as the girls open the refrigerator, they hear a door open upstairs.

⟳ Talk about It

- Why do people drink?
- Why do you think there is such an emphasis on drinking in this culture?
- What are some of the dangers of drinking?
- Is it a sin to drink? to get drunk?
- What would you do if you were in a situation like the one Jamie found herself in?

☑ Check It Out

Read Proverbs 23:29-35 and Proverbs 31:4-7 for a sobering reminder of the dangers of drinking alcohol.

♡ Apply It

Israel was a wine-producing country. In the Old Testament, winepresses bursting with new wine were considered a sign of blessing (Proverbs 3:10). Wisdom is even said to have set her table with wine (Proverbs 9:2, 5). But the Old Testament writers were alert to the dangers of wine. It dulls the senses; it limits clear judgment; it lowers the capacity for control; it destroys a person's efficiency. To use wine or other alcoholic drinks as an end in themselves, as a means of self-indulgence, or as an escape from life is to misuse them and invite the consequences that face the drunkard. The soothing comfort, the "highs," and the sense of belonging that you may get from using alcohol are only temporary. Real comfort, true "highs," and total belonging come only from a personal relationship with God, the creator of life. Don't lose yourself in alcohol; find yourself in God.

⛏ Tip for Parents

You cannot afford to ignore the topic of alcohol. Your kids will definitely face this temptation sooner or later (probably sooner). Figure out what values you want to communicate, and then sit down with your children and discuss the issue.

Angels

Whitney and her dad have just finished watching a popular TV show that features angels who go around helping people in trouble. All in all, it's a positive show—wholesome plots, mostly sweet characters, very sympathetic to the whole idea of spirituality. Every now and then, however, the show's writers include some unbiblical ideas about angels.

Take tonight's episode for instance. A boy died in the program and received an invitation to become an angel. But the ghostly boy was reluctant, even skeptical of such a calling. The show consisted of the boy's spirit accompanying an older angel on a special mission to help an elderly couple. In the end, the deceased boy realized how important angels are, so he agreed to undergo the transformation.

It made for a wonderful story. In fact, both Whitney and her dad were wiping their eyes at the conclusion. That's when Whitney turned to her father and asked, "Hey, Dad, do you think God will let *me* be an angel one day?"

○ Talk about It

- What are some recent TV shows, movies, or books that talk about angels? Which ones do you like best? Why?
- What do you know *for sure* about angels?
- Look up angels in a Bible dictionary. Read the article and discuss it. What surprises you? What facts contradict what you always believed?
- Why do you think angels have been so popular in the last couple of years?
- Angels are often portrayed in the works of famous artists as "babylike." What do you think is accurate or inaccurate about such a portrayal?

☑ Check It Out

For a biblical perspective on angels, consult Mark 13:27, 32; Psalm 148:2-5; and Colossians 1:16.

♡ Apply It

Angels are spiritual beings created by God who help carry out his work on earth. They praise God (Revelation 5:11-12), bring messages (Luke 1:26-28), protect God's people (Daniel 6:22), offer encouragement (Genesis 16:7-12), give guidance (Exodus 14:19), bring punishment (2 Samuel 24:16), patrol the earth (Ezekiel 1:9-14), and fight the forces of evil (2 Kings 6:16-18; Revelation 20:1). There are both good and bad angels (Revelation 12:7), but because bad angels are allied with Satan, they have considerably less power and authority than good angels. Eventually, the main role of the good angels will be to offer continuous praise to God (Revelation 19:1-3).

♟ Tip for Parents

If your children are asking questions about angels, a helpful resource is *104 Questions Children Ask about Heaven and Angels*. This clever, well-written book is a wonderful resource conceived and written by experienced parents.

Anger

Almost from birth, Tyler has had a very explosive temper.

As an infant, he would angrily scream and cry every time he was hungry.

As a toddler, he had a habit of throwing things—toys, food, whatever!—whenever he did not get his way.

As a preschooler, he sometimes pushed or hit other children.

Now, as a third grader, he continues to have problems exercising self-control. Just yesterday he got sent to his room. Storming back to the rear of the house, Tyler kicked open his door, went inside, and then slammed the door shut—so hard that it knocked two pictures off the wall in the hallway. Both pictures shattered.

Now Tyler's parents are angry—and frustrated. "What are we supposed to do?" asks Tyler's mom. "We have spanked and taken away privileges. We've read books and written letters to James Dobson. But nothing we try seems to work. When he gets angry, Tyler just loses control."

○ Talk about It

- What kinds of things make you the angriest? Why?
- How do you typically react when you feel really mad?
- Is it a sin to feel angry? Why or why not?
- What are some wrong ways to express angry feelings?
- What are some acceptable ways to express angry feelings?
- What advice would you give Tyler's parents?
- What would you tell Tyler if he asked you for some ideas on how to control his temper?

☑ Check It Out

Two great passages on anger (and how to deal with it) are Ephesians 4:26-27 and James 1:19-20.

♡ Apply It

Jesus got angry about the Pharisees' uncaring attitudes (Mark 3:5). Anger itself is not wrong. The rightness or wrongness of an angry response depends on what makes us angry and what we do with our anger. Too often we express our anger in selfish and harmful ways. By contrast, Jesus expressed his anger by correcting problems—healing a man's hand (Matthew 12:9-14) or restoring the temple courtyard to its purpose (John 2:13-16). Use your anger to find constructive solutions rather than to tear people down.

♟♟ Tip for Parents

Children need to be shown how to express anger in appropriate ways. Being destructive of things and being hurtful to others or to oneself are never acceptable. Some kids find they are able to blow off steam through physical exercise or manual labor. Others write in a diary or journal. One girl unwound by playing the piano really hard. Another screamed into her pillow until she felt better. Help your children find God-honoring ways to vent their feelings.

Animal Rights

The six o'clock newscast is showing live coverage of a huge animal-rights rally.

Protesters are gathered in a fashionable shopping district, holding up signs with such slogans as Pets are people too, Justice for all of God's creatures, No more vivisection, Cruelty-free cosmetics, and Stop animal research NOW!

Some animal-rights advocates are sitting in front of the doors of a cosmetics store. Their spokesperson is claiming that the makeup sold there is manufactured by a company that is cruel to animals.

The Emery family watches as police move in to break up the protest. Just then the camera catches a couple walking down the sidewalk together. The woman is wearing a fur coat. Suddenly, a bearded man runs up and throws a cup of what looks like blood all over the woman. The crowd cheers wildly, and a fight breaks out.

"Why are they doing all that?" eleven-year-old Megan asks her mom.

○ Talk about It

- What is your favorite kind of animal and why?
- What are the advantages and disadvantages of having a pet?
- Why are some individuals so passionate about animal rights?
- Many of the helpful medications and drugs that we use today were first tested on animals. What do you think about using animals in legitimate scientific research?
- Whose rights are most important—humans' or animals'? Why?

☑ Check It Out

Compare Genesis 1:28 and Proverbs 12:10.

♡ Apply It

In Matthew 10:29-31, Jesus describes God's care for his creatures. Yet he also explains that people are worth more than any of God's other creatures. At times people have valued financial gain above the value of either animals or other people. In the same way, some people value a cause more than they value the people who may disagree with their cause. When these things happen, cruelty of various kinds can result. While people may disagree on the topic of animal rights, God would have us remember two things: (1) Value the "sparrows," (God does), but (2) do not value those "sparrows" above people (God doesn't). God is aware of everything that happens, even to sparrows, yet you are far more valuable to him than they are. You are so valuable that God sent his only Son to die for you (John 3:16).

♟ Tip for Parents

There is a tremendous difference between treating animals with kindness and putting animals on an equal or greater level than human beings. Make sure your kids, in their natural affection for God's creatures, aren't deceived by the unbiblical claims of extremists.

Anxiety

Tryouts for the seventh-grade basketball team are tomorrow.

Denny is so nervous he can't eat or sleep. At school he's been daydreaming all week. He fantasizes about going up high to block the shot of the school's best player. Then he takes the ball the length of the court and does a reverse dunk. In the dream the coach stops practice to tell the other team members, "Men, did you see what Alexander just did there? I hope you did, because in ten years when he's playing in the NBA, you can say, 'That guy used to be on my junior high team!' That's how the game was meant to be played!"

Fantasies aside, Denny is as ready as he'll ever be. He and his dad have been practicing in the driveway for weeks. His foul shooting has improved dramatically. He's a good ball handler and a decent passer.

But there is still the issue of his size. Denny is shorter than most of the boys. He's quick but not very strong.

"How many boys did you say will be trying out?" Denny's mom inquires at supper.

"I'm not sure. About thirty."

"And how many are going to be picked?" she continues.

"Only fifteen."

"Fifteen! Well, you shouldn't have any problems then. That's one out of every two. Besides," she adds in a cheery voice, "you're the best little dribbler I know!"

Denny smiles weakly and nods even as he's thinking, *Mom, you don't have a clue. Every other guy, except for Matt Weaver, is taller than I am.*

That night Denny tosses and turns until almost 2:00 A.M.

○ Talk about It

- Why is Denny nervous?
- What's a situation in your life that you're worried or anxious about right now?
- What is the difference between anxiety and fear?
- Do you have a friend who's going through something like this?
- What can you tell your friend to help him or her?

☑ Check It Out

Read the words of encouragement God gave to Joshua as well as the encouraging words Joshua gave his men: Deuteronomy 31:8; Joshua 1:6-9; 8:1; and 10:25.

♡ Apply It

Planning for tomorrow is time well spent; worrying about tomorrow is time wasted. Sometimes it's difficult to tell the difference. Careful planning is thinking ahead about goals, steps, and schedules, trusting in God's guidance and protection. When done well, planning can help alleviate worry. Worriers, by contrast, are consumed by fear and find it difficult to trust God. They let their plans interfere with their relationship with God. Don't let worries about tomorrow affect your relationship with God today. Turn your fears, anxieties, and worries into prayer. Then leave them with God, trusting him for the outcome.

▐▌ Tip for Parents

Remember that situations that are "no big deal" to you may be very big deals to your kids. Make an extra effort to be sympathetic and empathetic.

Apathy

Classmates are excited about the party on Friday. But not Laura.

People are looking forward to the upcoming holidays. But not Laura.

Church members are eager to complete the annual "Yuletide Food Drive." But not Laura.

Family members are thrilled about next week's trip to Grandma's. But not Laura.

"What's up, Laura?"

"I don't know. I just don't really care about anything. I'm just kind of blah. I don't feel excited. I don't have any energy. I just want to lie around and do nothing for the next two weeks."

"But what about all the upcoming activities?"

"Maybe next year."

⟳ Talk about It

- Look up the words *complacent* and *apathy* in a dictionary. Discuss their meanings.
- What causes people to become complacent?
- What are some areas in your life where you find it difficult to get motivated or stay motivated?
- If a person honestly admits, "I just really don't care about _____," what can he or she do to change?
- What role does selfishness play in causing apathy?
- How is laziness tied to apathy?
- What advice would you give to Laura?

☑ Check It Out

Read about how God felt when the Israelites became complacent in their faith and unconcerned about anyone but themselves—Isaiah 32:9-11 and Amos 6:1-8.

♡ Apply It

In Luke 12:42-48, Jesus tells us how to live until he comes: We must watch for him, work diligently, and obey his commands. Such attitudes are especially necessary for people who have valuable gifts and abilities. The more resources, talents, and understanding we have, the more we are responsible to use them effectively. God will not hold us accountable for gifts he has not given us, but all of us have enough gifts and duties to keep us busy until Jesus comes. It is better to contribute *something* than not to contribute at all.

👫 Tip for Parents

We need to teach our kids the proper role of feelings in life. The Scriptures tell us to walk by faith (Habakkuk 2:4)—not feelings! At the same time, family members need to learn to communicate how they are feeling. This is critical if we are to understand and be sensitive to each other.

In short, talk about feelings and be aware of and sensitive to them, but do not let them dictate your family's activities.

Appearance

Here's a typical day in the life of the Mortley family:

6:57 A.M. Dave Mortley, thirty-nine, slips on his new suit jacket, adjusts his new tie, and stares at his image in the mirror. He turns sideways and sucks in his stomach. He's thinking about the afternoon meeting with Mr. Galloway and the old saying "You only get one chance to make a first impression."

7:11 A.M. Claire Mortley, fifteen, is looking in the mirror and is on the verge of tears. *Could I be any uglier?* she wonders. *Not only do I have to wear these* stupid *braces, but my complexion looks like a map of the moon!*

12:31 P.M. Liz Mortley, thirty-eight, glances again at the gorgeous young woman sitting at the table across from her. "Can you believe her?" Liz whispers to her lunchmate. "She's flawless!"

"I know! I know! I *hate* her!" is the sarcastic reply.

4:19 P.M. Mark Mortley, thirteen, is in the weight room with the rest of the freshman football team. When he realizes he's standing next to Pat Gill, the most muscular kid on the team, Mark feels embarrassed and slinks away to the other side of the room.

○ Talk about It

- What are some examples of our culture's obsession with appearance?
- Why does our society place so much emphasis on how we look?
- Is it ever wrong to worry about how you look? When?
- If you could wave a magic wand and change your appearance, what specifically would you change?
- Why do you think God gives some people exceptional good looks?
- Can you think of some ways in which being beautiful or handsome might be a *bad* thing?
- To what lengths should Christians go to improve or change their appearance? In other words, should a Christian color his/her hair? have plastic surgery? whiten his/her teeth?

☑ Check It Out

It's important to remember that God carefully created each one of us (Psalm 139) and that when he looks at us, he is far more concerned about how we look on the inside (1 Samuel 16:7).

♡ Apply It

You can't do much with the body you were born with—you can trim it and paint it, but it still looks pretty much like the original. But you can do a lot about what is on the inside. You can be as attractive as you want to be inwardly. You can have kindness, for example, in any amount you choose. You may not be able to control your looks, but you can control the attractiveness of your character.

♛ Tip for Parents

Do you compliment your children more on the way they look or on the way they act? We need to encourage and affirm our kids every chance we get—especially when it comes to behavior and character. By praising Christlike actions, we send out a strong and important message—who you are on the inside is far more important than how you appear on the outside!

Arguing

It's just before mealtime and everyone is cranky.

The baby is fussing.

Mom is trying frantically to get dinner on the table.

Dad is complaining about the electric bill that arrived in the day's mail.

And the twins are arguing about everything. They've been yelling at each other ever since they got home from school.

Right now the fight is over who gets the Winnie-the-Pooh placemat.

"*I* got it out."

"So what! Grandma gave it to *me.*"

"No, she didn't!"

"Did too!"

"Did not!"

"Well, then *I* get the red crazy straw."

"That's mine! You broke *your* straw!"

"MOM!"

○ Talk about It

- Is it automatically wrong to get into an argument? Or is it possible to disagree and still do it in a way that honors God?
- What causes family members to argue over such silly little matters?
- What was the last argument you had? What was it about? What finally happened?
- What are some better ways to solve conflicts than simply yelling at each other?
- How do you feel when you are in an argument?
- How do you feel when you see other people argue? Why?
- Do you think Jesus argued with his brothers and sisters? Why or why not?

☑ Check It Out

Read the good reminders in Philippians 2:13 and Proverbs 15:1-2.

♡ Apply It

Have you ever tried to argue in a whisper? It is very difficult; our natural bent is to raise our voice as we argue. It also takes great effort to argue with someone who keeps on answering calmly and gently. A gentle answer tends to calm us down (Proverbs 15:1). And a rising voice and harsh words almost always trigger an angry response. Try to turn off the argument and invoke peace by choosing to use gentle words whenever an argument threatens to break out.

▮▮ Tip for Parents

Many newlyweds (and "oldyweds") suffer because they have never learned proper conflict-resolution skills. They simply do what they saw their parents do—raise voices, storm out of the room, clam up, change the subject, etc. Don't perpetuate the cycle. Let your home be a laboratory where your children can learn how to disagree in a way that honors God.

Astrology

Shelby can't figure her friends out. They're so silly the way they run around saying, "What's your sign?" and "I'm a Taurus. What are you?"

Every day they read their horoscopes in the paper. And today Marcy has a book full of predictions "based on the stars."

"OK, Shelby, listen to this. Your Capricorn reading for today says, 'Be careful in conflict. If you overreact you will find trouble, but if you suppress your emotions, you will experience great blessing.' Well, what do you think?"

"I think you guys are stupid! Why don't you go buy a bunch of fortune cookies? At least you can eat those."

"You're so negative! And I don't see why. This stuff really works! It's totally accurate!"

"No, it isn't. It's totally *vague*. You can interpret *anything* that happens to you to fit those ambiguous statements."

"Well, you can be skeptical if you want. All I know is that this is really helping me deal with life."

☾ Talk about It

- What do you think about people who consult astrologers and read horoscopes?
- What's the difference between astronomy and astrology?
- Do you know anyone who is into psychics or palm readers? What is his/her explanation for why he/she does that?
- Why do you think people are so eager to consult the stars and so reluctant to consult (through prayer) the One who made the stars?
- What about looking at horoscopes "just for fun"? Should Christians do that? Why or why not?

☑ Check It Out

Read the warnings found in Deuteronomy 4:19; 17:2-3; and Isaiah 47:13-14.

Apply It

Most people would like to know the future. Decisions would be easier, certain failures would be avoided, and some successes would be assured. In Jeremiah's day, the people of Judah wanted to know the future too, and they tried to discern it through reading signs in the sky. Jeremiah explained how misguided that approach was (Jeremiah 10:2-3). God made the earth and the heavens, including stars that people consult and worship (10:12). No one will discover the future in made-up charts of God's stars. But God, who promises to guide you, knows your future and will be with you all the way. He may not reveal your future to you, but he will be with you as the future unfolds. Don't trust the stars; trust the One who made the stars.

▮▮ Tip for Parents

Oftentimes parents let "teachable moments" slip away. For instance, a commercial for the psychic hotline comes on TV, and Mom hurries to change the channel so little Susie won't see it. Try this approach next time you see such an advertisement: Ask your child(ren), "What do you think about that? Do you think just by looking at the stars, someone can tell us our future?" Start a discussion. Listen. Then teach. We can only protect so much. At some point we have to teach our children to think and to discern.

Authority

When Nick gets home from school, he's holding a folded-up piece of paper.

"What's that?" Mrs. Nadeau inquires, a puzzled look on her face.

"Um, it's a, um . . . well—it's a . . . see, what happened is that . . . well, it wasn't all *my* fault. Mrs. Bardin was just in a bad mood, and so that's why I, um . . ." Nick is clearly uncomfortable, shifting his weight from one foot to the other, refusing to make eye contact.

"Why don't I just read it for myself?" Mrs. Nadeau finally interrupts, taking the note.

It's from the principal of Nick's school. Apparently Nick smarted off to a teacher on duty in the lunchroom. When asked to move to a different table, Nick responded by saying something like, "You're not my mom. You can't tell me what to do."

Mrs. Nadeau gently takes Nick's face and forces him to look into her eyes.

"Did this happen? Did you say that to that teacher?"

"Well, *she* said I was causing trouble. That I threw a roll at another kid. But I didn't! Mom, I promise! And so I didn't think it was fair that *I* should be the one to have to move."

"OK, OK. I believe you. But did you *say* that?"

Nick looks down, kicks at the carpet with his foot, and nods uneasily.

"Nick, you know better than that. When you're at school, you have to do what the teachers say."

"But Mrs. Bardin's mean! Nobody at the whole school likes her!"

"That doesn't matter. She's in charge. Like it or not, you *have* to do what she says."

○ Talk about It

- What's an "authority"? Give some examples from your own life.
- Talk about an authority figure you don't mind obeying and one you hate obeying. What makes the difference?
- In what ways is authority a good thing? What would happen if everybody ignored their parents, teachers, bosses, and even the government?
- What do you think might happen to Nick?
- What is the secret to submitting to (or obeying) authority figures?

☑ Check It Out

Consider how the Bible urges us to respond to the following authorities: government (Romans 13:1-6), church leaders (Hebrews 13:17), employers (Ephesians 6:5-9), and parents (Ephesians 6:1-4).

♡ Apply It

During the time of the judges, the people of Israel experienced many years of great trouble because everyone became his own authority and acted on his own opinions of right and wrong (Judges 21:25). All they had to do was submit to God. But they had a knack for rebelling against authority, so they suffered greatly. Usually it took them a long time to see the mistake of their rebellion and submit themselves again to God. We should take heed. When individuals, groups, and societies make themselves the final authorities without reference to God, when people selfishly satisfy their personal desires at all costs, everyone pays the price. No one can afford it.

♛ Tip for Parents

As in so many areas of life, our children's attitudes about authority will be affected by how they see us respond to those to whom we are subject. We can talk about submitting humbly to those who are over us, but if we don't do it, our words will be empty. Be careful what you say about government officials, law-enforcement personnel, and your employer.

The Bible

GOD'S INSPIRED BOOK

Todd has a friend who reads the Bible every day. This friend even goes to a weekly Bible study with other teenagers. At the friend's church (Todd visited a few times), the pastor preaches from the Bible every week. Basically these people act like the Bible is the most important book in the world.

But Todd has lots of questions: "How come my teachers at school never mention the Bible? Why does the local bookstore have thousands of books but only one rack of Bibles (and it's way in the back of the store)? How come at my church the minister barely refers to the Bible but instead just tells inspiring stories?"

Here's how Todd sums up his dilemma: "I guess I'm just trying to figure out what's so special about the Bible. Why do some people get so excited about it, while others act like it's just another book?"

☯ Talk about It

- What *is* so great about the Bible?
- Some books are inspiring; the Bible claims to be inspired (2 Timothy 3:16-17). What's the difference?
- Some people say, "The Bible is God's revelation to the world." What does that mean?
- Do the members of your family treat the Bible as God's Word? Why or why not?
- What would you say to Todd if he were your friend?

☑ Check It Out

For an accurate reminder of the true nature of the Scriptures, read Isaiah 40:8; 1 Thessalonians 2:13; and 2 Timothy 3:16-17.

♡ Apply It

The Bible is not a collection of stories, fables, myths, or merely human ideas about God. It is not a human book. Through the Holy Spirit, God revealed his person and plan to certain believers, who wrote down his message for his people (2 Peter 1:20-21). This process is known as *inspiration* (2 Timothy 3:16). The writers wrote from their own lives and experience. Although they used their own minds, talents, languages, and styles, they wrote what God wanted them to write. Scripture is completely trustworthy because God was in control of its writing. Its words are entirely authoritative for our faith and lives. The Bible is God's inspired Word. Read it and use its teachings to guide your conduct.

Tip for Parents

Many kids complain that the Bible is too hard to understand, irrelevant, or boring. That may be because they're reading a version that is intended for adults. Take advantage of these great resources: for small children, *The Eager Reader Bible;* for older children, the *Kid's Application Bible;* for teens, the *Life Application Bible for Students.* Each of these is filled with age-appropriate charts and notes that will enable readers to understand and apply God's Word.

The Bible

Can the Bible really make a difference in a person's life? Just ask the members of the Watson family:

Father Charles has been memorizing Scripture with some other men from the church. "I've found that when I get into tempting situations, I'm able to call certain verses to mind that give me a right perspective. I feel more powerful to resist sin."

Mother Jenny is in a women's Bible study, and she says, "I feel my faith deepening. I really trust God more than I did even a couple of months ago. The more I read and study, the more I truly believe that God can and will do great things. I'm praying more and seeing him work."

Daughter Casey claims, "I've been facing some big decisions, and I feel like God's Word has helped guide me. It doesn't say specifically 'Go to this college or that one!' but I've gathered some really good principles that have helped me see what choices are best."

Daughter Carolyn has learned how to share her faith by doing a study of how Jesus talked to people. "I never knew how to witness until we did this Bible study. Now I don't feel so clueless when my friends ask me questions about God."

○ Talk about It

- What's your favorite Bible book? verse? character? Why?
- If you have ever memorized Scripture, quote a verse for the rest of your family.
- How has the Bible helped your faith grow? Give an example.
- How has the Bible helped you make a decision? Explain.
- Talk about a way in which the Bible has equipped you to be a better Christian.
- If people spied on you for a month (put a hidden video camera in your room, followed you around, etc.) what would they conclude about your beliefs regarding the Bible?

☑ Check It Out

Read these verses that specify how the Bible can make a difference in your life—Psalm 119:11, 105; 1 Peter 2:2; and Hebrews 4:12.

♡ Apply It

One psalm writer said that he was a "foreigner here on earth" and needed guidance (Psalm 119:19). Almost any long trip requires a map or guide. As we travel through life, the Bible should be our road map, pointing out safe routes, obstacles to avoid, and our final destination. We must see ourselves as pilgrims, travelers here on earth who need to study God's map to learn the way. If we ignore the map, we will wander aimlessly through life and risk missing our real destination.

▮▮ Tip for Parents

The more our children see us reading the Bible and valuing it and seeking wisdom from it and relating it to life, the more they will come to trust it as the precious resource that it is. Don't be like families who treat the Scriptures like an ancient artifact in a museum display. Pull it off the shelf daily (at times other than these devotions!), and get your whole family interacting with it. By the way, are you attending a good church where the Bible is preached? John Stott once said that preachers should preach with the Bible in one hand and a newspaper in the other. That idea also applies to parents. Let your kids see that the Bible really does relate to everyday life.

Bitterness

In Sunday school, Sharon, Sheila, and Leslie have always liked to sit together, whisper, and pass notes. When old Miss Grantham was their teacher, they did it easily, and she never even noticed. Now, however, Mrs. Boyd is the new sixth-grade girls' teacher. And Mrs. Boyd is pretty strict. She doesn't allow talking, and she sure doesn't tolerate passing notes.

Three weeks ago, after warning the girls twice, Mrs. Boyd suddenly announced, "All right, Sheila, that's it! Give me the note. I'm not going to let you disrupt this whole class. Go sit over there by yourself. And maybe while you're over there, you can think about what you're going to say to your parents after I tell them how you've been acting."

Well, needless to say, Sheila got in big trouble at home. And ever since then, she has kept quiet in Sunday school. However, Sheila refuses to look at or speak to Mrs. Boyd. Her reasoning? "I can't stand her! She got me in trouble. I'll never forgive or forget what she did!"

✑ Talk about It

- Can you think of some instances in your life when someone did something to make you really mad? What happened?
- Why do you think Sheila got so mad at Mrs. Boyd? Did Mrs. Boyd do anything wrong? If so, what? What is Sheila doing wrong?
- How would you describe bitterness? Is it the same as not being willing to forgive?
- What causes some people to get extremely bitter while others never seem to hold grudges?
- What should Sheila do? What do you think might happen if she continues to refuse to forgive Mrs. Boyd?

☑ Check It Out

Look at what God tells us to do with feelings of bitterness—
Ephesians 4:31.

♡ Apply It

Jesus taught that whoever hates another person is a murderer at heart (Matthew 5:21-22). The apostle John echoed that idea years later (1 John 3:15). Christianity is a religion of the heart; outward compliance alone is not enough. Bitterness against someone who has wronged you is an evil cancer within you and will eventually destroy you. Don't let a "bitter root" (Hebrews 12:15) grow in you or your church.

♟ Tip for Parents

Help your children understand that holding a grudge only hurts the one who is unforgiving. Someone has said that bitterness is like holding onto a hot coal. The tighter and longer you hold on, the worse it will scar you. The best way to pass this lesson on is to make sure you are not modeling a bitter attitude toward anyone or any situation.

Blaming

Melanie Leonard is making taco salad for lunch. Her husband, Lyle, offers to shred the cheese. Mark, ten, volunteers to get the chips and hot sauce out of the pantry. Little Jan, six, decides she wants to get in on the act, so she runs to the refrigerator and gets the new package of cheddar for her dad.

Lyle sets his bowl and grater on the edge of a narrow strip of counter. Melanie foresees trouble. "Lyle, uh, I don't know if you'll have room to work there."

"Mel, I'm just grating some cheese—there's plenty of room here." Then, turning to Jan, Lyle says, "OK, open the package."

Melanie is frowning. "Lyle, I just swept and mopped."

"What? You must think I don't know anything about cooking and kitchen stuff." Lyle is irritated. "Jan!" he snaps. "Don't unwrap the cheese so much! You can just leave it in the package. Here—give it to me."

He grabs the cheese with all the flair of Betty Crocker. He's ready to show what he can do. Picking up the grater, he begins shredding the cheese. After grating about half the package, he looks up at his wife and smirks. Just then his wrist hits the bowl of cheese and sends it crashing to the floor.

"Lyle!" Melanie snaps. "I told you that was going to happen!"

Lyle is embarrassed and humiliated. "Well," he blusters, "it wouldn't have happened if Jan hadn't unwrapped the cheese so much!"

⟳ Talk about It

- In the story above, who is to blame for the spilled cheese? Why?
- How do you think Jan feels?
- How do you think her dad feels?
- Why do we so commonly blame others for the mistakes we make?
- If someone wants to get out of the habit of blaming others, what are some practical ways to do it?

☑ Check It Out

See the first instance of one person blaming another in Genesis 3:1-13.

♡ Apply It

When God asked Adam about his sin, Adam blamed Eve. When God turned to Eve, she blamed the serpent. How easy it is to excuse our sins by blaming another person or the circumstances! People often try to avoid guilt feelings by shifting the blame. Excuses include: (1) It's the other person's fault; (2) I couldn't help it; (3) everybody's doing it; (4) it was just a mistake; (5) nobody's perfect; (6) the devil made me do it; (7) I was pressured into it; (8) I didn't know it was wrong; and (9) God is tempting me. A person who makes excuses is trying to shift the blame to something or someone else. But this won't solve the problem. Besides, God knows the truth, and he holds each of us responsible for what we do. A Christian should not try to get away with a wrong act by blaming someone else. Admit wrong attitudes and actions, apologize to God (and to anyone you may have blamed), accept responsibility, and ask God for forgiveness.

▮▮ Tip for Parents

Think back on your week. If you have been guilty of unjustly blaming your child, ask for forgiveness. You'll be amazed at how a humble admission of wrong on your part can strengthen your relationship.

Boredom

Saturday morning, the O'Neills wake to the dreaded sounds of thunder and rain.

"Great!" Jonathan squawks. "It's pouring down rain. They can't have the carnival in weather like this!"

"Not rain!" moans his older sister Kim as she emerges from her bedroom. "Our bike hike will be canceled for sure!"

"Who cares about some dumb bike trip!" snaps Jonathan.

"I do!"

"You can bike anytime."

"So, you can have a stupid carnival anytime."

"Kids!" Mrs. O'Neill can tell it is not going to be a fun day. "It's not even 9:00 A.M., and y'all are already at each other's throats. Cool it!"

"Well, what am I gonna do now that the school carnival is off?"

"You could clean your room."

"Mom, I'm serious!"

"So am I."

Kim tries a different approach. "Mom, will you take me to the mall later?"

"Why do you need to go to the mall? You went Thursday night."

"I don't know. . . . I sure can't sit around here."

"Why not?"

"I don't know. It's boring here. There's absolutely nothing to do."

"Don't you have homework?"

"I did it all in study hall yesterday afternoon."

"Well, maybe we can all do something together. In fact, let's try to think of someone we can help, since we seem to have a whole day on our hands!"

"Huh?" Jonathan and Kim respond—almost in unison.

○ Talk about It

- When are you the most bored and why?
- What do you usually do when you're bored—complain? clean your room? watch TV? call a friend? something else?
- What would you do if you could plan out your ideal day?
- What do you think about Mrs. O'Neill's suggestion about doing something for somebody else?
- What are some ideas for things you could do—individually or as a family—next time you're facing a "boring" day?

☑ Check It Out

Read Galatians 6:9-10 and apply it to the common complaint "There's nothing to do!"

♡ Apply It

The Holy Spirit gives Christians great power to live for God. Some Christians want more than this. They want to live in a state of perpetual excitement. But lots of days are filled with normal activities, sometimes even boring ones. When you face one of those days, ask God's Spirit to stir you up. Every day offers a challenge to live for Christ.

Tip for Parents

Consider putting together a "Rainy Day Plan" so that you don't get caught off guard the next time the weather alters your intentions.

Borrowing

"Mom!"

Mrs. Campbell can tell by the tone (not to mention the volume) of her fourteen-year-old son's voice that he is extremely irritated.

"What, Roy?"

"He did it again."

"Who did what?"

"Billy took my Dolphins cap without asking. It's gone. He's gone. Now I don't have anything to wear."

"Why don't you wear your Notre Dame cap?"

"It's all bent out of shape."

"Well, what about your Braves cap?"

Roy is horrified. "Mom, it's not baseball season!"

"What if you wore one of Billy's caps?"

"Oh, right! Like I'm going to wear a Buffalo Bills cap! Or a Mighty Ducks cap! Nobody wears those caps! Mom, the point is that he takes my stuff all the time without asking. I want him to stop doing it."

"OK. I'll have a talk with him when he gets home. But before you get too carried away, let me ask you a question: Whose sweatshirt do you have on?"

Roy gulps. The Chicago Bulls sweatshirt he's wearing belongs to Billy.

"Billy said he doesn't care if I wear this."

"Then why do you get so upset if he borrows your cap?"

⟳ Talk about It

- How do you feel about letting your brother or sister (or someone else) borrow things that belong to you?
- Which is easier for you to lend someone—clothes? favorite toys or games? money?
- Why is it easy to share certain things and hard to share others?
- What rules does your family have about borrowing and sharing?
- What should be the consequences for a family member who borrows something without asking?

✉ Check It Out

How does Matthew 7:12 relate to this discussion?

♡ Apply It

The words in Matthew 7:12 are commonly known as the Golden Rule. In many religions it is stated negatively: "Don't do to others what you don't want done to you." By stating it positively, Jesus made it more significant. We ought to refrain from harming others; at the same time, we also should take the initiative in doing something good for them. The Golden Rule as Jesus formulated it is the foundation of active goodness and mercy—the kind of love God shows to us every day. Believers in Christ should show this kind of love in their dealings with others. Consider the way of love the next time you want to take a particular action. Ask, "Is it loving? Is it kind? Would I want someone to do this to me?"

⫯⫯ Tip for Parents

Teach (and model for) your children the important biblical truth that everything we have belongs to God. He owns it all, and we are to manage it wisely. Such an approach prevents us from becoming stingy and selfish.

Career

A large group of kids is discussing that age-old question: "What are you going to be when you grow up?"

Eric says he wants to be an airline pilot.

Caleb talks about being a builder like his dad.

Jhru wants to play professional basketball.

Leigh Anna says she's going to be a dancer.

Patrick wants to work on computers like his dad.

Kelly says she wants to be a mommy.

Zack dreams of being an astronaut . . . or maybe a policeman.

Right now it's fun to think about doing big things. And there's no great pressure to make a decision. Each child will probably change his or her mind a hundred times.

But when they get to be older, they'll have to give serious thought to this important question. What they decide to do in life will determine what courses they take in high school, if and where they go to college, and what classes they sign up for once they get there.

No wonder so many people worry about that question!

◯ Talk about It

- (For kids) What do you think you want to be when you grow up?
- (For parents) When you were little, what did you want to be?
- What are some jobs you would never want to do? Why?
- What is a career?
- What are some ways we can try to figure out what career is best suited for us?
- Should people choose a job solely because of how much money it pays? Why or why not?

☑ Check It Out

The Bible doesn't specify what careers we should pursue, but it does give us guidelines. Read these passages and state the principle contained in each: 1 Corinthians 10:31; Matthew 6:33; Acts 1:8; and 1 Peter 4:10-11.

♡ Apply It

As a young apprentice in the tabernacle, Samuel "became the Lord's helper, for he assisted Eli the priest" (1 Samuel 2:11). In this role, Samuel's responsibilities would have included opening the tabernacle doors each morning (1 Samuel 3:15), cleaning the furniture, and sweeping the floors. As he grew older, Samuel assisted Eli in offering sacrifices. He wore a linen ephod (a garment worn only by priests) as a priest-in-training (1 Samuel 2:18). Because Samuel was Eli's helper, he was God's helper too. When you serve others—even in carrying out ordinary tasks—you are serving God. Because ultimately we serve God, every job has dignity.

▮▮ Tip for Parents

The older our kids get, the more we seem to worry about grades and college and the future. Why? Because we want to see our children find careers that honor God and bring fulfillment (not to mention putting food on the table!). What can we do? We can and should pray for God's guidance. We should seek to provide opportunities for our kids to experience different kinds of work. And we should strive to instill in them a willingness to work hard. Figuring out *where* to work is easier when one is experienced and knows *how* to work.

Cheating

The history fair is tomorrow, and Greg Cook's project should easily take home a prize. It is a scale model of the Alamo—so detailed it looks like it belongs in a museum. The only problem with Greg's project is that Greg didn't do it. His dad did.

The situation began with Greg doing the work and Mr. Cook offering advice. But each night, Greg's dad became more and more involved. The last couple of nights, Greg was barely able to contribute at all. His dad basically took over, leaving Greg to sit at the table pretending to be involved while watching the sports channel out of the corner of his eye.

Greg knows the model looks great—perhaps too great. But he feels guilty about not having done the work. He wonders if his teacher is going to say something. He wanted his dad's help—he really did. He just never thought his dad would totally take over.

On the phone that night, he asks his friend Tim what to do.

"I wish my dad cared enough to help me. Man, I say you ought to be glad you have a decent project. You might even win the fair! Wait till you see mine. It's a piece of junk. I threw it together in two nights. Quit stressing!"

○ Talk about It

- Was it right for Greg's dad to do Greg's project for him?
- What could Greg have said to his dad?
- Should parents help kids with school projects?
- What's the difference between acceptable help and so much help that it amounts to cheating?
- Does cheating ever pay off? Why or why not?

☑ Check It Out

Read Proverbs 10:2; 16:8; and 20:23. Show how they might apply to situations where a person is tempted to cheat.

♡ Apply It

Proverbs 20:23 describes how the Lord "despises" the loaded scales a merchant might use in order to cheat the customers. In other words, God hates all kinds of dishonesty. Dishonesty is a difficult sin to avoid. It is easy to cheat if we think no one else is looking. But dishonesty affects the very core of a person. It makes him untrustworthy and untrusting. It eventually makes him unable to know himself or relate to others. Don't take dishonesty lightly. Even the smallest act of dishonesty contains enough of the poison of deceit to kill your spiritual life. If there is any dishonesty in your life, tell God about it and ask him to help you get rid of it.

▮▮ Tip for Parents

It's important for parents to be involved with their kids' schoolwork and to be available to help as needed. But parents need to guard against taking over as Greg's dad did in this story. Talk with your children about acceptable, appropriate levels of help with their schoolwork and how they can communicate with you about the amount of help they need or want.

Chores

It's getting close to bedtime at the Benda household.

The dishes are in the dishwasher. The kitchen has been cleaned. Baths have been taken. And now, before the bedtime ritual of reading and telling stories, the rest of the house needs to be tidied up.

"Catherine, the TV room is really messy tonight. You go pick up in there, and Tyler and I will straighten up the living room."

"But, Mom!"

"Catherine, I don't want to hear any complaining. Just do what I asked."

"But, Mom, Tyler's the one who made most of this mess. Why should I have to clean up his mess?"

"Because we're a family and we help each other out. I didn't dirty your dishes tonight, but I cleaned them up. I don't dirty your clothes every day, but I wash them."

"Well, it's not fair."

"Well, that's too bad. You do it anyway, or we won't be reading any books tonight."

☯ Talk about It

- What chores do you have to do? Which ones do you like and dislike? Why?
- What's it like at your house when it's time to do chores?
- Do you ever feel like Catherine in the story above?
- Is Catherine's mom being unfair? Why or why not?
- What are some messes you make that others end up having to clean up or take care of?
- How could picking up and cleaning up actually be *fun?* Is that possible?

☑ Check It Out

Note that when the people of Israel set about the task of rebuilding the city's walls, everybody got involved—Nehemiah 3:6-12. No one (except for the lazy men of Tekoa, see verse 5) said, "Wall building is just not my specialty!" On the contrary, they all pitched in, and the monumental task was completed in less than two months!

♡ Apply It

Crossing the Red Sea was only the beginning. Years later, after wandering in the wilderness for forty years, the Israelites had a Promised Land to conquer. And that included land on both sides of the Jordan River. The twelve tribes had to divide up this land after it was conquered. Yet the hard work was done by all of the tribes together. The tribes of Reuben and Gad and the half-tribe of Manasseh did not stop after their land was cleared; they promised to keep working with the others until everyone's land was conquered (Numbers 32:16-19). After others have helped you, don't make excuses to escape helping them. Finish the whole job, even those parts that may not benefit you directly.

♟ Tip for Parents

It seems that each generation is lazier than the one before. The builder generation (people who experienced the hard times of World War II) is recognized for its commitment to hard work. But their children, the baby boomers, reveling in the good times of the post-war economic boom, failed to fully embrace that ethic. Now, the baby buster or so-called Generation X age group has largely lost any sense of working hard and saving and sacrificing. We need to restore a commitment to the value of hard work in our country. And that can only begin in our individual homes.

Christmas

In early October, Brad and Jeannie Beier are surprised to find Christmas decorations beginning to fill the local mall. Red bows. Candy canes. Posters of Santa. Even the faint sounds of holiday carols emanating from a few stores.

All of this raises a question that the Beiers have been pondering for some time: How should they celebrate the season? Specifically, how will they resolve the secular "Santa" version of Christmas with the biblical "baby Jesus" version?

Brad, in his typically logical manner, analyzes the situation. "Well, the way I see it, we really only have two options: We can totally avoid any mention of Santa Claus. A lot of our friends at church do that. They talk only about the birth of Jesus."

"And I understand that, believe me!" Jeannie nods. "Each year everything gets more and more secular and more and more materialistic. I sure don't want our kids to grow up thinking Christmas is all about a man in a red suit who gives you whatever you ask for. But at the same time, we have to be realistic. Whether we like it or not, they're going to get bombarded with images and stories about Santa. It's unavoidable."

"I know, I know. So the other option would be for us to emphasize the Bible story of Christmas but to also tell the truth about St. Nicholas—who he was, and how, at least according to tradition, he was a Christian who helped others and gave them presents."

"Would that really work?"

Brad shrugs and smiles. "I don't know. You tell me."

○ Talk about It

- What do you like best about Christmas? Least?
- What is the true meaning of Christmas?
- How can families avoid going overboard in talking about Santa Claus?
- Is it wrong to talk about Santa Claus at Christmastime? What if it plays only a small part in a family's Christmas celebration?
- What does your family need to do in order to preserve the true meaning of Christmas?

✉ Check It Out

Read Luke 2:1-20 for an ever important reminder of what happened on that first Christmas.

♡ Apply It

At Christmastime we often think of Jesus as a baby in a manger (Luke 2:7), but that scene alone tells only part of the story. The Christ child in the manger—the tiny, helpless baby of Christmas cards and nativity scenes—grew up. He lived a perfect life, died for us, ascended to heaven, and will come back to this earth as King of kings. He will rule the world and judge all people according to their decisions about him. Do you still picture Jesus as a baby in a manger—or is he your Lord? Make sure you don't underestimate Jesus. Let him grow up in your life. Make Christmas a time of celebrating his rule as well as his coming.

♀♀ Tip for Parents

One family found a solution to this "holiday quandary" by telling their children the true story of St. Nicholas and then saying, "Over the years, people changed his name to Santa Claus, and they like to pretend he still brings presents, but the *truth* about Christmas and what it *really* means is that God gave the world the best present of all—a Savior named Jesus." Talk with Christian friends you respect and admire. Find out what they do (if you don't already know) and why they choose to celebrate in that fashion. Ultimately, you will have to develop your own convictions in this area in which Christians have so many different beliefs.

Church Unity

For the last three weeks, the telephones of the members of Valley Church have been especially busy. Why? Because the church is in the middle of a huge conflict over its pastor. One group in the congregation loves Reverend Nelson. The other group is ready to send him packing. At a church business meeting last week, things got terribly heated. Ugly words were said. Accusations were made. Tempers flared.

Now it looks as though the church may split apart! At least thirty families are threatening to leave. "If Reverend Nelson stays," declared a leader of the opposing faction at the meeting, "then we leave!"

At Sunday lunch, the Holliday children are filled with questions. "I don't understand all this," says Justin. "I thought Christians are supposed to love each other. What about unity? What about forgiveness?"

"I know," pipes in Lauren. "It was really weird in our Sunday school class today. Some of the kids won't talk to each other. They just sit there and glare at each other. And I'm talking about two girls who just last month were *best friends.*"

Toya looks at Shawn, and they both just shake their heads. Toya remembers a painful church split she went through as a teenager. It got really ugly. Almost twenty years later, she *still* can't believe some of the things people in her church did and said to each other.

Shawn finally speaks. "Kids, all I know to do is to pray really hard for people to do right. And even if people act ugly and say mean things, we need to make sure that we act like Jesus."

"I know that's what we're supposed to do," Justin admits, "but it's hard to love people when they're saying bad things about Reverend Nelson."

◯ Talk about It

- What do you think about the situation at Valley Church?
- Why do Christian people sometimes get so angry at each other?
- When would it honor God for a family to leave a church? Why?
- How do you think you would respond if you were in a situation like the one the Hollidays are facing?
- What can you do this week to express your love and support for your pastor?

☑ Check It Out

Read Colossians 3:12-17 and Ephesians 4:1-6 for a look at how Christ wants his church to behave.

♡ Apply It

"We are all one body," wrote the apostle Paul (Ephesians 4:4). Unity does not just happen; we have to work at it. Often differences among people can lead to division, but this should not be true in the church. Instead of concentrating on what divides us, we should remember what unites us: *one* body, *one* Spirit, *one* hope, *one* Lord, *one* faith, *one* baptism, *one* God! Have you learned to appreciate people who are different from you? Can you see how their differing gifts and viewpoints can help the church as it does God's work? Learn to enjoy the way we members of Christ's body complement one another. (See 1 Corinthians 12:12-13 for more on this thought.)

▮▮ Tip for Parents

Make sure your children hear you speaking positively of your church and its leadership. If you are negative and critical, then they will learn to be suspicious as well. Though no church or pastor is perfect, we are called to honor those who lead us spiritually. Let your kids see that practice at work in your home.

Clothes

Just before the beginning of school, the Dilberts go on their annual clothes-buying excursion. In the past, Mrs. Dilbert has always dictated what clothes Marcy and Mandy could get. Not this year.

For the first time, Mrs. Dilbert is giving each girl a sum of money to spend pretty much as she wishes. "It's time you girls learned how to shop around and find the best deals for yourselves. I'll go with you, and I'll be glad to give you my advice, but this year you make the decisions."

In the first department store, Mandy finds a pair of designer jeans that she loves. Immediately she announces, "I'm getting these!"

"But don't you want to look around a little bit?" Marcy asks.

"Why keep looking when you've found something perfect?"

"Well," Marcy points out, "you might find them cheaper somewhere else. Or you might even find a good sale on some other brand and end up getting two pairs for the same price you'd be paying here for one."

"I don't want some cheapo brand. I want *these*. All my friends are wearing them."

○ Talk about It

- Who is the best dresser in your family? Who is the best shopper?
- Do you prefer to be dressed up, casual, or sloppy in your clothing? Why?
- Why do some people get so concerned about having the "right" brands of clothing?
- How much emphasis do *you* put on clothes and what to wear? Why do you think you do that?
- What can you tell about a person by looking at the clothes he or she wears?

☑ Check It Out

Read Matthew 6:28-33 for a reminder about how important clothes are in the eternal scheme of things.

♡ Apply It

We should not be obsessed with fashion and outer beauty. It goes without saying that we should take care of ourselves and give proper attention to hygiene, neatness, and grooming. But even more important are a person's attitude and inner spirit (1 Peter 3:3-4). To develop these takes time and energy. If we become obsessed with external beauty, we will lose perspective and the ability to make wise choices. Remember: True beauty begins inside.

❙❙ Tip for Parents

Many parents set limits on how much they will spend for an item of clothing. For instance, a mom says, "I will give you up to forty dollars for new tennis shoes." Junior then knows that if he wants a hundred-dollar pair of Nikes, he has to come up with the other sixty dollars himself. Not only does this system teach children the value of money, but it can motivate them to work hard and to save for what they want.

Commitment

It's only two weeks into the new softball season, but Blair wants out.
"It's no fun. We just stand around in the hot sun. And besides, our team is terrible. I'm quitting."

"Blair," says her father firmly, "you're *not* quitting."

"Why not? I don't like softball anymore."

"Well, that may be so, but you made a commitment to play."

"So?"

"So, that means you need to stick it out. Your team is counting on you. And you need to learn that when you agree to do something, you don't turn right around and change your mind. You have to fulfill your obligations."

"But, Dad, I hate it! And besides, Marcy said she's quitting, too."

"Look, I'm sorry. I can't control what Marcy does. If her parents let her quit, I think that's a big mistake."

"But why?"

"Blair, listen. You may not understand this right now, but life is filled with situations that are hard and unpleasant. And you can't always walk away from those situations just because you decide you don't like it anymore. People who adopt that attitude end up leaving churches and getting divorces. Why? Because they aren't willing to follow through on their commitments."

"Gee, Dad! Who said anything about divorce? I just want off this cruddy softball team."

◌ Talk about It

- What is commitment? How would you define the word?
- What are some situations in life where you have to do things you don't want to do?
- In what ways should Christians be committed?
- What would the world be like if nobody was committed to anything?
- How can you strengthen your commitment to Jesus today?

☑ Check It Out

Read about how the disciples stayed committed to Christ even when a lot of his other followers walked away—John 6:60-69.

♡ Apply It

Everyone wants to be a hero and receive praise, honor, and wealth. But as royal Persia saw firsthand, few are willing to pay the price (see the book of Esther). Mordecai served the government faithfully for years, bore Haman's hatred and oppression, and risked his life for his people. Haman had no time for such humility. The price to be paid by God's heroes is long-term commitment, with no claim on the prize. Are you ready and willing to pay the price?

▮▮ Tip for Parents

In a world of fickle people who live solely by feelings—spouse swappers, job hoppers, and church shoppers—we need to instill in our children a solid understanding of commitment. Without a clear grasp of the meaning of terms like *dedication* and *devotion,* how will they know that marriage is for life and that debts must be paid (not dismissed through legal means) and that promises have to be kept, even when it hurts?

Teach this and model it, and you will do the world a huge service!

Comparisons

It's not easy being the kid brother of Carol Aswell.

Carol is a brain. She's never made a B in her life. Her teachers love her, and they remind Barry of that fact all the time. (He would be *thrilled* to make all Bs.)

Carol is multitalented. She plays piano and sings really well. She can also act and cook. Barry, on the other hand, is talented primarily in the area of playing video games.

Carol is outgoing and popular. She's always being elected "class favorite" or "class secretary," and she belongs to a number of clubs.

Not Barry. He's painfully shy and has only two or three friends.

Barry's parents try not to compare him to his sister, but sometimes they can hardly help themselves. They just wish he would get excited about *something.*

⟳ Talk about It

- Why do we compare people?
- What are the dangers of being compared? of comparing ourselves to others?
- How do you feel when you are compared to someone who's more talented, smarter, prettier, etc.?
- Are comparisons *always* bad? Why or why not?
- Does God compare? How do you know?
- In your family, are comparisons a common thing or not? Talk about how you feel about this.

☑ Check It Out

Read the familiar story found in 1 Samuel 17:32-40. Note especially that David felt no obligation to try to be like Saul.

♡ Apply It

When you do your very best, you feel good about the results. There is no need to compare yourself to others. People make comparisons for many reasons. Some point out others' flaws in order to feel better about themselves. Others simply want reassurance that they are doing well. When you are tempted to compare, look at Jesus Christ. Ask only whether you are striving toward his goals for you (Galatians 6:4). Set your sights on his example. This will inspire you to do your very best, and his loving acceptance will comfort you when you fall short of your expectations.

♟ Tip for Parents

This is no great revelation, but every child is different. Each one is a unique masterpiece. Our goal as parents is to help our children be the people God made them to be, not the people we think *we* would like them to be. To do this successfully we must become students of our children. We must understand their individual personalities, strengths, and weaknesses. Don't press your children into molds when God is clearly in the business of breaking molds.

Competition

Trey Decker loves just about everything about baseball. He loves his new batting gloves. He loves striking out an opposing player. He loves standing at the plate and connecting with a fastball that is low and outside. He enjoys sitting in the dugout during games and joking around with his teammates.

The only unenjoyable aspects of summer baseball for Trey are the way his dad acts when he coaches the team and the way his mom acts when she watches his games from the bleachers.

Trey's dad takes the game way too seriously. He seems to think his team should be able to duplicate the fielding and baserunning of a major-league franchise. He chides the players when they goof up; and when *Trey* makes a bad pitch or throws to the wrong base, Mr. Decker pulls him aside and reams him out in a muffled yet stern voice.

Trey's mom is equally competitive—and even more vocal. She cheers the players on in a loud, shrill voice, and she frequently protests umpire decisions. Way out in center field, you can hear her above all the rest of the fans.

For Trey, it's embarrassing. "I want to win as much as anybody," he insists, "but, after all, it is just a game. And it would be a whole lot more fun if my parents would lighten up. None of the other guys have parents who go so overboard about baseball."

⟳ Talk about It

- Are you a competitive person or not?
- What makes some people so much more competitive than others?
- When is competition OK, and when does it go too far?
- Why do some parents push their children so hard to succeed in sports (or academics or music or anything else)?
- What are some ways Trey could ask his parents to lighten up?

☑ Check It Out

How does Galatians 6:4 speak to the whole issue of competition?

♡ Apply It

Games are fun, and it's always more fun when we play—in a friendly manner—to win. But we can't win all the time. Nor is it necessary. Just the excitement of the game and the thrill of pushing ourselves to our limit should be enough to have fun.

❚❚ Tip for Parents

Every now and then play games without keeping score. We don't always have to end up with "winners and losers" in order to have a good time. Play just for the enjoyment of playing. Your kids will appreciate the change of pace.

Complacency

A visiting preacher spoke at First Church this past Sunday on the return of Christ. He pounded the pulpit, he strode back and forth across the platform, he raised his voice, and toward the end of his message, he even broke down and cried. It was a very good message, but it failed to move some of the members of the youth group. Here's a snatch of their conversation after the service:

"So, what did everybody think of the guest preacher?" sixteen-year-old Kelly asked. (She thought he was great.)

Her friend Andrea commented, "I thought he made some good points. I didn't care for all his theatrics, but I thought his message was pretty good."

Jason wasn't so charitable, however. "I don't understand why so many preachers harp on that subject. They've been predicting the end of the world for centuries now. It's even in the Bible—all these warnings about 'get ready, the end is near.' But look—here we are almost two thousand years later, and life is still going on like normal. If you ask me, I think a lot of preachers use messages like that to try to scare people."

Kelly is rather surprised. "You sound like you don't believe Jesus is coming back."

"I never said that," Jason objects. "I just said I wish some preachers wouldn't harp on it so much."

"But don't you think we need to think about it more often? How else will we be ready if the Lord *does* come back?"

"That's true, Kelly, but you have to get on with life, too. There is such a thing as being so heavenly minded, you're no earthly good."

○ Talk about It

- Do you agree with Jason's comments?
- If you were Kelly, what would you say to Jason?
- How might it change our behavior if we truly believed Jesus might come back anytime?
- Do you feel ready for heaven? Why or why not?
- How can we help each other remember that Jesus is coming back soon?

✉ Check It Out

Read Ezekiel 12:21-28 for an important reminder that what God has said will come to pass.

♡ Apply It

The two short messages recorded in Ezekiel 12:21-28 were warnings that God's words would come true—soon! Less than six years later, Jerusalem would be destroyed. Yet the people were skeptical. Unbelief and false security led them to believe it would never happen. The apostle Peter dealt with this problem in the church (2 Peter 3:9). It is dangerous to say Christ will never return or to regard his coming as so far in the future as to be irrelevant today. God is not slow; he just is not on our timetable (Psalm 90:4). Jesus is waiting so that more sinners will repent and turn to him. We must not sit and wait for Christ to return, but we should live with the realization that time is short and that we have important work to do. Be ready to meet Christ anytime, even today, yet plan your course of service as though he may not return for many years.

♟ Tip for Parents

Ask your pastor to recommend a good, readable book on the end times. A great fictional treatment of the subject is *Left Behind* by Tim LaHaye and Jerry Jenkins. This topic is of interest to kids of all ages, and reading such a book together might prove to be a good family project.

Complaining

Things were not very pleasant at the Hamptons' home last night.

The unhappiness began when Mrs. Hampton served another one of her meat-stretcher recipes—this one called something like Tuna Breadcrumb Surprise. "Mom!" ten-year-old Jeremy protested. "This stuff is gross!"

"Yeah," added thirteen-year-old Jonathan. "The *surprise* is to see whether or not you can keep it down."

Mrs. Hampton slammed down her fork. "All right, that's it—you both can leave the table!"

Later that evening, Jonathan began grumbling about not having anything to wear to school. "*Nobody* dresses like me. I look like a misfit. I look like I got all my clothes from Wal-Mart."

Mrs. Hampton looked at him with daggers in her eyes. "We *did* get most of your clothes at Wal-Mart. So what? What's wrong with that?"

Jonathan rolled his eyes, shook his head, turned, and stomped down the hallway to his bedroom, where he cranked up his radio.

"Mom," Jeremy yelled, "tell him to turn it down! How am I supposed to do my homework?"

Jonathan poked his head out of his room. "Oh yeah, right! Like you've *ever* done homework in your whole pathetic life!"

"Boys!" Mrs. Hampton screeched.

Later, when the boys were asleep, Mrs. Hampton called her mom, who lives out West.

"Are you OK? Is anything wrong?" her mom asked worriedly.

"Oh, Mom, everything's wrong! I'm so frustrated, I could spit!" she began. And with that she launched into a fifteen-minute tirade about how crummy her life was.

☯ Talk about It

- What things really get on your nerves? What do you tend to complain about most?
- Why are we more likely to focus on the negative things in our lives than on the positive things?
- Do adults and children complain about the same things or different things? Why?
- What could the Hamptons do to improve the situation in their home?
- What could you do to help make your home a "complaint-free" zone?

☑ Check It Out

God takes a dim view of those who grumble and complain—see Numbers 11:1-10.

♡ Apply It

The Israelites complained, and then Moses complained, but God responded positively to Moses and negatively to the rest of the people (Numbers 11:1, 11-15). Why? The people complained *to one another,* and nothing was accomplished. Moses took his complaint *to God,* who can solve any problem. Many of us are good at complaining to each other. We need to learn to take our problems to the One who can do something about them.

👥 Tip for Parents

Complaining is, like most behavior, habit-forming. That is, if we do it regularly, it becomes almost second nature. The antidote is cultivating the opposite habit of gratefulness. By concentrating on the good in our lives, we become less bothered by life's annoyances. Make your premeal prayers less ritualistic and more genuine. Have each family member say one or two things he or she is thankful for. This can become a beloved family tradition.

Confession

When Mr. Alexander turned on his computer last night, something was wrong. He couldn't find several documents he had been working on and needed to finish. *That's weird,* he thought. *I know they were right here in this folder.*

Using the "find" command, he finally located two of them—in a folder marked "games." The other two were nowhere to be found.

Mr. Alexander got up from the desk and went into the living room. "Josh, have you been playing on my computer?"

Josh immediately got a guilty look on his face. He gulped. "No, sir," he lied.

"Are you sure? Because I can't find two of my documents. They're gone. And two others somehow ended up in the *games* folder."

"Um, no, Dad!" Josh lied again. "I don't know how that could have happened. Maybe Jared did something."

Josh felt bad all night. He couldn't get to sleep. He wanted to go tell his dad the truth, but he was afraid of what the consequences would be if he did.

○ Talk about It

- How do you feel when you do something you know is wrong?
- When in your life have you felt the guiltiest? What happened?
- What does it mean to confess your sins? Why is that important?
- When is it necessary for us to confess our sins not just to God but also to other people?
- What do you think Josh should do?
- What will happen if Josh confesses? What if he doesn't tell?

☑ Check It Out

Read about the importance of confessing your sins to God in Psalm 32:1-5 and 1 John 1:9.

♡ Apply It

We need to make a habit of confession because we tend to make a habit of doing wrong. The longer we delay confession, the more damage our backed-up sin can do (Psalm 66:18). Whenever you confess, listen to God and express your desire to stop doing what is wrong. David confessed his sin and prayed, "Cleanse me from these hidden faults. Keep me from deliberate sins!" (Psalm 19:12-13). When we refuse to repent or when we harbor and cherish certain sins, we place a wall between ourselves and God. We may not be able to remember *every* sin we have ever committed, but our attitude should be one of confession and striving to change.

▮▮ Tip for Parents

It is hard for us to swallow our pride and admit to our children when we have blown it. Nevertheless, this is one of the best lessons and examples we can give our kids. If they grow up seeing us humble ourselves and admit fault, it may make it a little easier for them to do the same. Is confession a part of your family life?

Confidence

It's about one minute until the curtain rises for the big Christmas play. Standing side by side at center stage are Emily and Lauren, best friends and the two main characters in the production.

Emily is so nervous, she's about to hyperventilate. She's whispering frantically, "Lauren, what if I forget my lines? What if I trip? What if I forget to do something I'm supposed to do?"

Lauren tries to calm her. "Shhh! Just relax, Emily. You know your lines. We've practiced this thing until we could do it in our sleep! Now forget about all the people out there and just enjoy yourself! Ham it up and have fun."

"Oh, Lauren, I don't get you. How can you be so relaxed?"

"I don't know. I guess I feel like I did my part, and now God is going to do his."

○ Talk about It

- Talk about a time when you felt extremely scared or nervous. What was the problem? What eventually happened?
- Do you tend to be more like Emily or Lauren? Why?
- What do you think about Lauren's advice and her philosophy?
- What is the difference between having self-confidence and having confidence in God?
- What are some situations coming up in your life that you don't have a lot of confidence about?
- How does God's faithfulness affect our confidence?

☑ Check It Out

Read about the great confidence of Caleb—Numbers 13:25-31 and 14:5-9.

♡ Apply It

Self-sufficiency is an enemy when it causes us to believe we can always do what needs to be done all by ourselves, without God's enabling. To prevent this attitude among Gideon's soldiers, God reduced their number from thirty-two thousand to three hundred (Judges 7:2-8). With an army this small, there could be no doubt that victory was from God. The men could not take the credit. Like Gideon, we must recognize the danger of striving in the belief that we act alone. We can be confident of victory only if we put our confidence in God and not in ourselves.

♟ Tip for Parents

A lot of parents do things to try to boost the self-confidence of their children. We need to make the effort to boost their confidence in God. Every time you remind your kids of God's power and faithfulness, and every time they see you actively and genuinely trusting God, you do something wonderful for them—you give them a gift with long-term benefits!

Conflict

Jeremy comes home on Friday and reveals to his wife that he'll be playing in a golf tournament on Saturday.

Instantly, Angie's pleasant demeanor changes. The cheerful conversation in the kitchen dissipates. The atmosphere in the room becomes highly charged.

"You know," Angie begins, "I think it's interesting the way you just announce these things. You don't bother to ask if it is convenient for me. You don't check to see how it might fit with my schedule. You just make these decisions, and then you announce them to me."

"Oh, come on, Angie!" Jeremy protests. "You know I need to unwind on the weekends. I work like a dog all week long."

"So do I!" Angie snaps. (She's losing it!)

"So?" Jeremy can't think of anything else to say.

"So, it irritates the heck out of me that you can just plan your life, and I always have to bend and flex to accommodate your schedule. Now it's golf. Next month it'll be fishing. In the winter it'll be hunting. You just do whatever you want, and I have to deal with it!"

Jeremy can feel himself getting angry. "So what is it that you want?"

"I want you to think about me for a change. I want you, just once, to stop and say, 'Pete, before I make these plans, let me check with Angie and see how this fits with her needs and her schedule.'"

Jeremy is not sure what to say, but Angie is just getting warmed up. "How would you feel if every weekend, the minute you walked in the door, I just announced to you, 'Oh, honey, by the way, the girls and I are going shopping all weekend'? Or if I said, 'Dear, I forgot to tell you, but a bunch of us are going to a cooking class each Saturday for the next month'?"

By now Jeremy's face is red. The kids, Hillary and Emery, can sense a coming explosion. They quietly slip out of the room.

○ Talk about It

- What causes conflicts?
- Is conflict a sin?
- What situations cause the biggest conflicts in your family? Why?
- What rules should families make regarding conflicts?

☑ Check It Out

How does 1 Thessalonians 5:13-15 relate to this discussion about conflict resolution?

♡ Apply It

Have you ever tried to argue in a whisper? It's pretty hard to do! It is equally hard to argue with someone who insists on answering gently. On the other hand, a rising voice and harsh words almost always trigger an angry response. To turn away wrath and seek peace, choose gentle words.

Tip for Parents

It is imperative that our children understand that conflict is a fact of life—even among committed Christians. Our concern should not be whether we will have conflicts (if we are normal and honest, we will) but whether we will resolve our conflicts in a God-honoring way. Teach your children this skill, and you have given them an ability that is priceless for relational success.

Consequences

After a Fourth of July cookout with the neighbors, the Hardy family is sitting wearily in their living room discussing the outing.

"Can you believe those Osigian kids?"

"I know. I think you could safely say they've missed a few spankings. They're out of control."

"Yeah, but I blame the parents for that."

"Oh, I know! They're oblivious. They're sweet people, but they're just terrible parents. They don't watch their kids. And then when they *do* see them do something, they don't say a word! I watched Mark shove little Carol over in the sandbox and take her bucket. And Dean was sitting right there, and he never corrected him."

"Well," fourteen-year-old Carrie announces, "they're just a little bit strange if you ask me. Any family that would keep nine cats and let them run all over the house and shed all over the furniture—I'm sorry, but I just find that weird."

Suddenly the Hardys hear a knock at the screen door leading to the back porch. It's Dean Osigian! He's bringing back some grilling tools he borrowed for the cookout.

The embarrassed Hardys are wondering if he heard their discussion. It's hard to tell from looking at him. He doesn't seem mad, but then, he's not real friendly, either.

Dean departs, leaving the Hardys feeling sick to their stomachs.

☯ Talk about It

- Have you ever been in a situation like the one described above? What were the circumstances and what happened?
- How would you have felt if you were one of the Hardys?
- How could the Hardys have avoided getting into such an uncomfortable situation?
- What is the lesson from this incident?

☑ Check It Out

Read Numbers 32:23 and Galatians 6:7 for an important message about the consequences of sin.

♡ Apply It

Galatians 6:7 says that people will reap what they sow. In other words, it would certainly be a surprise if you planted corn and pumpkins came up. It's a natural law that each kind of seed sown will grow that particular kind of plant. This law of nature has applications in other areas of life, too. Every action has results. If you gossip about your friends, you will lose their friendship. If you plant to please your own desires, you'll reap a crop of sorrow and evil. If you plant to please God, you'll reap joy and everlasting life. What kind of seeds are you sowing?

♟ Tip for Parents

The next time you watch a TV program, talk about the plot and whether it is realistic. Ask your children to discuss the potential consequences of the actions of the show's characters.

Contentment
WITHOUT ENVY

The Ronald Dunn family is returning from a visit with the Charles Dunn family. (Ronald is Charles's younger brother.) Because Charles is a prominent—and prosperous—physician, his family lives a very privileged life. Their house is huge, gorgeous, and situated on a hill overlooking the seventh green at the Bentwood Golf & Tennis Club.

Charles's children attend a prestigious private school. They have lots of expensive toys (go-carts, four-wheelers, computer games, etc.). Charles's wife, Kristin, is very polished and maintains a gorgeous figure (from her daily games of tennis at the club).

In the car, Ronald and his family are comparing their lifestyle to that of Uncle Charles and his family.

Ronald thinks their own house is a tiny, little dump.

Ronald's wife, Pat, feels like a fat slob.

The kids are jealous of all the clothes and gadgets their cousins enjoy.

"Dad, when are we going to get a new car?"

"There's nothing wrong with this car. It's only four years old."

"Yeah, but compared to Aunt Kristin's—"

"Look, I don't want to hear any more about Aunt Kristin's car! It's a pretty car. But it ought to be for what they paid for it!"

For the next thirty miles, no one says a word.

◯ Talk about It

- Why do you think Ronald Dunn and his family felt so irritable and restless after visiting their relatives?
- What about your own life are you not contented with? Why? How would you change this if you could?
- Why do we tend to focus on what we don't have instead of what we do have?
- What is the secret to contentment? Or, in other words, what advice would you give Ronald, Pat, and their family?

☑ Check It Out

Read Paul's perspective on contentment in Philippians 4:10-13.

♡ Apply It

Are you content in any circumstance you face? Paul knew how to be content whether he had plenty or whether he was in need. The secret was drawing on Christ's power for strength. Are you discontented because you don't have what you want? Learn to rely on God's promises and Christ's power to help you be content. If you always want more, ask God to remove that desire and teach you contentment in every circumstance.

We must remember the difference between our *wants* and our *needs*. We may not get all that we want. But whatever we truly need on earth God *will* supply, even if it is the courage to face death as Paul did. By trusting in Christ, our attitudes and appetites can change from wanting everything to accepting his provision and power to live for him.

▮▮ Tip for Parents

The next time you sense your family being discontented, try the "thanksgiving exercise." Have the members of your family take turns thanking God for various things in your life—spiritual, relational, emotional, and material blessings. If you'll spend fifteen or twenty minutes doing this, you'll be amazed at the change it will make in your attitude!

Contentment
DESPITE LIFESTYLE PRESSURES

When the Langs bought a lot in the exclusive Turtle Creek subdivision, they did not imagine the kind of pressure they would feel to copy the lifestyle of their neighbors. Some examples:

The Langs originally were planning to build a house with 2,400 square feet. They had found "perfect" plans eight years before, a layout that was exactly what they wanted and needed in a home. But when they discovered that the smallest house in the neighborhood was 2,900 square feet, they suddenly found themselves back in the architect's office, adding a guest suite off the rear of the main house.

Art has been driving his Chevy pickup for fifteen years and 185,000 miles. He really loves it, and there's not a thing in the world wrong with it—except that it looks pretty shabby. Lately Art has been noticing that the other men in Turtle Creek are driving nicer, newer vehicles. Suddenly Art is seriously shopping for some new wheels.

For the last six years, the Lang children have had a blast going to summer camp at Piney Point Ranch. It's not fancy, but it's a great place, full of good memories. However, their new Turtle Creek friends are now showing them cool videos of Camp Attakkapau, a state-of-the-art, very pricey camp in the Blue Ridge Mountains. Suddenly, Andrew and Katherine have no interest in Piney Point. All they can talk about is going to Attakkapau this summer.

⟳ Talk about It

- What does it mean to "keep up with the Joneses"?
- How would you explain the change of attitudes in the members of the Lang family?
- What are some things your neighbors or friends are able to enjoy that you wish you had? Is it wrong for you to feel that way? Why or why not?
- What does it mean to be content?
- What is the secret of contentment?
- The Bible is very clear that things will not last and that we are to lay up treasure in heaven (Matthew 6:19-21). If this is true, why do we get so obsessed with having things, and why do we pay so little attention to "heavenly treasure"?

☑ Check It Out

Trying to "keep up with the Joneses" is dangerous to your spiritual health. See 1 Samuel 8:19-20 and 2 Kings 17:15.

♡ Apply It

Jesus said that the good life has nothing to do with being wealthy, so be on guard against greed—desiring what we don't have (Luke 12:15). This is the exact opposite of what society usually says. Advertisers spend millions of dollars to entice us to think that if we buy more and more of their products, we will be happier, more fulfilled, more comfortable. How do you respond to the constant pressure to buy? Learn to tune out expensive enticements and concentrate instead on the truly good life—living in a relationship with God and doing his work.

▐▌ Tip for Parents

Just by being in the world, our children will naturally desire more and more things. But we can fight materialistic urges by doing three things: (1) by creatively showing our kids that it's possible to have fun without buying lots of stuff; (2) by limiting the amount of time they are allowed to wander through toy stores (or watch commercials) and lust for new playthings; (3) by spending time with healthy families who share our determination to be content.

Convictions

When Suzanne and Cindi were kids, they squabbled as most friends do. As adults, their disagreements have taken on a different dimension. Now they spar because of conflicting convictions, and their opposing viewpoints sometimes create tension when their families get together. Some examples:

Cindi's kids grew up believing in Santa Claus. Suzanne can't believe a Christian family would advocate that.

Suzanne won't shop on Sunday. Cindi doesn't see what the big fuss is.

Suzanne's family pulled the plug on their TV last year. Cindi thinks that is "a bit extreme."

Suzanne's girls will not be allowed to get their ears pierced until they are fourteen. Cindi's daughter had hers done at age eight.

Suzanne's kids are forbidden to listen to many styles of "contemporary Christian music." Cindi is thrilled that her kids want to listen to "Christian music rather than the trash on the radio."

With all their differences, it is amazing that Suzanne and Cindi even have a friendship. But somehow they do.

✪ Talk about It

- What are some things that you feel strongly about and why?
- Reviewing the story above, what are your convictions in each of the areas mentioned?
- How do you go about determining what your convictions will be?
- How should we respond when friends or relatives have different convictions?

☑ Check It Out

For some excellent principles on developing convictions in the areas of life where the Bible gives no clear direction, read Romans 14:1-12.

♡ Apply It

Differences of opinion need not cause division. They can be a source of learning and richness in our relationships. Believers ought to act according to their conscience, but their honest scruples do not need to be made into rules for everyone else. Certainly some issues are central to the faith and worth fighting for—but many are based on individual differences and should not be legislated. Paul warned in Romans that we are not to quarrel about issues that are matters of opinion. Our principle should be: In essentials, unity; in nonessentials, liberty; in everything, love.

♟ Tip for Parents

Try to help your child(ren) understand the difference between biblical standards and cultural norms. For example, many Christians avoid friendships with unbelievers, believing such interaction to be spiritually dangerous. But nowhere does the Bible teach against building redemptive relationships. Therefore, this common practice of noninvolvement with non-Christians is more cultural than it is biblical.

Creation

In one recent week, the Orillion girls were bombarded with ideas about the world and how it began.

On Earth Day, the girls listened to a speaker at a school assembly talk about "our living planet." She was very passionate and funny. But when she answered students' questions after her speech, she kept referring to "Mother Earth." And some of the literature she brought with her talked repeatedly about the "goddess Gaia."

In Sunday school the girls watched a video about the Creation. It was well made and very interesting. The video pointed out many of the flaws in evolutionary theory—the lack of fossil evidence and some questionable scientific techniques, as well as the scientific community's bias against God. The only thing Joanna and Shelly weren't sure about when they left was the much-debated question about the age of the earth. Joanna is convinced that the earth is young—only about six thousand years old. Shelly is skeptical. "I think it could be millions of years old and not conflict with what the Bible says."

On public television that same week, the girls watched a program about the Serengeti in Africa. The show was filled with references to evolution and our "apelike" ancestors.

○ Talk about It

- Why is the origin of the earth and of the human race such an important issue?
- How can Christians care about the earth without worshiping the earth?
- How should Christians respond when the fact of Creation is attacked?
- What parts of the Bible's account of Creation leave you puzzled?
- Can evolution and Creation both be true at the same time? Why or why not?

✉ Check It Out

The Bible states plainly that God created the world and all that is within it—see Genesis 1:1; Psalm 19:1; and Nehemiah 9:6.

♡ Apply It

The simple statement that God created the heavens and the earth (Genesis 1:1) is one of the most challenging concepts confronting the modern mind. The vast galaxy we live in is spinning at the incredible speed of 490,000 miles an hour. But even at this breakneck speed, our galaxy still needs 200 million years to make one rotation. And there are over one billion other galaxies just like ours in the universe.

Just how did God create the earth? This is still a subject of great debate. Some say that there was a sudden explosion, and the universe appeared. Others say God started the process, and the universe evolved over billions of years. Almost every ancient religion has its own story to explain how the earth came to be. And almost every scientist has an opinion on the origin of the universe. But only the Bible shows one supreme God creating the earth out of his great love and giving all people a special place in it. In this life we will never know all the answers to how God created the earth, but the Bible tells us that God did create it. That fact alone gives worth and dignity to all people.

👫 Tip for Parents

There are some terrific books in print about the Creation, written just for kids. In a world that advocates so many unbiblical views about the origins of the universe, you might want to invest in a couple of the better books available. Try *Wonderful Earth!* by Nick Butterworth and Mike Inkpen and *It Couldn't Just Happen: Fascinating Facts about God's World* by Lawrence Richards.

Death

It happened suddenly, without warning, on a hot, lazy July afternoon. In a single moment the Caston family came face-to-face with the fragility and brevity of life.

Carla, eight, was standing in the driveway with Patches, the family mutt, when a fire engine, siren wailing, came roaring up the street.

Patches, not normally a car-chasing dog, took off after this strange, loud, red monster. Mrs. Caston walked out the front door just in time to see Patches stumble and slide right under the wheels of the speeding pumper engine.

As the fire engine continued toward its destination, the female members of the Caston family rushed out into the street. Carla was already sobbing by the time they reached their beloved pet. He quivered, shook, and then became unusually still.

By this time Mrs. Caston was crying, too.

"Is he going to be OK, Mom?"

"No, baby, I'm afraid not. I think Patches is dead."

"But we could take him to the vet! Hurry, Mom, go get the car!"

"Oh, baby, I wish the vet could help him. But Patches is gone."

Carla sobbed louder. "But I want him! I don't want him to go! Why did it happen, Mom? Why?"

Mrs. Caston grabbed her daughter and gave her a long tight hug. "I don't know, baby. I don't know."

◯ Talk about It

- What person or pet who has died do you miss the most and why?
- What are some ways to help someone who is sad over the death of a loved one?
- In view of the fact that we will all die one day (and none of us knows when), how should we live today?

☑ Check It Out

Read 1 Corinthians 15:21-28 for a good reminder about how death affects believers in Christ.

♡ Apply It

The resurrection of Christ is the center of the Christian faith. Because Christ rose from the dead as he promised, we know that what he said is true—he is God. Because he rose, we have certainty that our sins are forgiven. Because he rose, he lives and represents us to God. Because he rose, we know we will also be raised. All Christians, including those living when Christ returns, will live with Christ forever. Therefore, we need not despair when loved ones die or world events take a tragic turn. God will turn our tragedies to triumphs, our poverty to riches, our pain to glory, and our defeat to victory. All believers throughout history will stand reunited in God's very presence, safe and secure. We should comfort and reassure each other with this great hope.

Tip for Parents

Having a pet can teach children good lessons about life and death. Many parents have used the death of a pet to talk about grief as well as to talk about eternal life in Christ.

Debt

The bigger the Witmer kids grow, the smaller the Witmer residence seems. That explains why the family is thinking hard about buying a bigger house.

After looking at dozens of new and "preowned" homes, the Witmers at least know what they want: a four-bedroom, two-and-one-half-bath house with two separate living areas. One of the homes on the market (2,500 square feet, only three years old, and in a great new neighborhood) fits the bill quite nicely.

Explains Pat: "The fourth bedroom could double as a study/guest room. And having a living room *plus* a den/family room means we can have small group or youth meetings and not have to banish the rest of the family to the back of the house. And isn't the deck just gorgeous!"

Gorgeous or not, the problem is money. The Witmers' current home is tiny (1,400 square feet)—with a corresponding mortgage. This new home would mean monthly payments almost twice what they are paying now. Bigger payments would require cutting the family budget in other areas and possibly finding some extra income from other sources.

It's a huge commitment, but as Pat notes, "It's also a gorgeous house!"

↻ Talk about It

- How do you think it would change the Witmers' life if they bought the new house?
- What does it mean to be in debt? How does it feel to be in debt?
- What is *interest?*
- What happens to people who take on too much debt?
- What happens when people can't pay their debts?
- Why is it important for families to discuss and set spending priorities and goals?

☑ Check It Out

The Bible cites several principles that can apply to decisions about borrowing money and buying things. See Proverbs 22:7; Luke 12:15 and 14:28; and James 4:13-16.

♡ Apply It

It is easy to get into debt and hard to get out of it. Every debt brings with it pressure to delay or even avoid repaying it. But any delay or default can have serious consequences. If the money came from a friend or family member, it can destroy trust and divide even the closest people. If you must borrow, be as eager to repay your loans as you are to get them, and pay them back ahead of schedule if possible. Then discipline yourself to be content with what you have so you don't have to borrow again.

👥 Tip for Parents

If we don't teach our children about money, we do them a grave disservice. Many Christian financial consultants agree that it is wise for parents to teach their children to save their money first and then make purchases. Otherwise, they assert, our children will buy into the cultural practice of "getting it now and paying for it (dearly) later." You also may want to set up a small loan for your children to teach them important lessons about debt and interest and repaying loans. Seizing a bike for nonpayment may sound cruel, but the lessons gained would ward off even greater pain later on in life!

Decisions

Life is full of decisions. Some are no big deal: What shirt should I wear? What toy should I play with? What friend can I call? What snack should I eat?

But other decisions are hard. Consider the situations that face the members of the Veerman family.

Mr. Veerman is trying to decide whether to buy into a duck lease. It's a hunter's paradise, but it also costs five hundred dollars. Should he spend that much money on a hobby when the family has other needs? *Gail really wants that new sofa, but hobbies are important, too! And it's not like I go out and splurge on myself all the time,* he thinks to himself.

Sons Michael and Daryl are wondering whether to go on a scouting trip this weekend or to the birthday party of a kid in the neighborhood who doesn't have many friends. Their parents have left the decision up to them.

Daughter Claudia is debating an invitation to the school dance. She was hoping Justin would ask her, but out of the blue Ty called. She's supposed to let Ty know something tonight. "I don't want to hurt his feelings, but at the same time, I'd really rather go with Justin. . . . But what if I turn Ty down and then Justin doesn't call?"

○ Talk about It

- What are some of the toughest decisions you've ever faced?
- What did you eventually decide to do?
- What are some of the worst decisions you ever made? What went wrong?
- How do you go about making decisions—that is, what criteria do you use?
- What advice would you give to the people in the story above?
- What is one tough decision you are facing right now? (One by one, let your family members give you some advice.)
- How would it change your decision making if you made it your goal in each situation to try to do whatever Jesus would do?

☑ Check It Out

Because Jesus was so close to his heavenly Father, and because he was so committed to doing the right thing, he always made good choices. See John 5:19-20 and 8:29.

♡ Apply It

"If you need wisdom—if you want to know what God wants you to do—ask him, and he will gladly tell you" (James 1:5). By *wisdom,* James means not only knowledge but also the ability to make wise decisions in difficult circumstances. Whenever we need wisdom, we can pray to God, and he will generously supply what we need. Christians don't have to grope around in the dark, hoping to stumble upon answers. We can ask for God's wisdom to guide our choices.

Wisdom also means practical discernment. It begins with respect for God, leads to right living, and results in increased ability to tell right from wrong. God is willing to give us this wisdom, but we will be unable to receive it if our goals are selfish. To learn God's will, we need to read his Word and ask him to show us how to obey it. Then we must do what he tells us.

♟ Tip for Parents

Introduce your children to the best-selling novel *In His Steps* by Charles Sheldon. The story focuses on some average church members whose lives are radically changed when they begin making every decision by first asking the question "What would Jesus do?"

Depression

The Peatross family doesn't know what to do with Shawna. She's not herself. Over the last few weeks she's said very little, she's eaten very little, and she's become very lethargic. She keeps mostly to herself and resists efforts by family members to engage in activities she really enjoys.

The other kids have picked up on the fact that Shawna seems to be battling a case of the blues. Allison has left little notes and surprises for her big sister. Alan has (to his parents' total shock) been very loving—even giving his bummed-out sister a number of hugs!

Last night Shawna went to bed early, and the family talked about her situation.

"She's acting weird, Mom," said Alan, stating the obvious.

"I know, I know. I'm worried about her."

"Maybe we should see a counselor," Mr. Peatross suggests.

"I think we need to do something."

"I'll make her a card!" little Allison chirps.

"That would be very sweet, honey," Mrs. Peatross concludes.

✪ Talk about It

- What causes people to get depressed?
- Have you ever felt blah or hopeless or totally lifeless? What do you think made you feel this way? How did you get over it?
- What are some ways people wrongly try to snap out of their depression?
- How can God help during bouts with depression?
- What would you do if you were a member of the Peatross family?

✉ Check It Out

What insights do these Scriptures—Psalm 13:1-2 and 34:18—bring to the subject of depression?

♡ Apply It

Depression is one of the most common emotional ailments. One antidote for depression is to meditate on the record of God's goodness to his people (Psalm 42:5-6). That will take your mind off the present situation and give hope that it will improve. It will focus your thoughts on God's ability to help you rather than on your inability to help yourself. When you feel depressed, take advantage of God's antidepressant. Read the Bible's accounts of God's goodness, and meditate on them.

♟ Tip for Parents

It's important to remember that depression may be caused by chemical imbalances or genetic tendencies. If a family member is demonstrating any of the following patterns—low self-esteem, sudden weight gain or loss of appetite, a desire to sleep excessively, loss of energy, unusual patterns of withdrawal, feelings of hopelessness—it is wise to consult your family physician. Left untreated, depressed individuals can spiral downward quickly, sometimes with tragic consequences.

Devotions

Colleen and Casey Tilley are not looking forward to supper tonight. Yesterday their mother announced that they were going to begin having a family devotional time after supper every Thursday.

"I wonder if this is going to be as bad as the last time we tried having family devotions. Do you remember that magazine Dad read from? It's like it was written by some old guy in a monastery somewhere. And the picture on the front of it looked like it was from the forties."

"Casey, it wasn't just bad, it was terrible! And do you remember how long each one lasted? It seemed like those things went on for hours!"

That night after supper, Mr. Tilley pulls out a new book. Colleen is curious. "Hey, Dad," she says, "before we start, can I look at that for a minute?"

"Sure."

Colleen eagerly takes the book and begins thumbing through it. She is pleased to see that each devotional is short. And each one deals with a different topic—most of them very interesting. She begins skimming one story on fashion, and immediately she can relate.

"Hey," she says to no one in particular, "this looks pretty good."

"Your dad and I think you're going to like it."

After reading a short scenario, the Tilleys have a good time discussing a few short questions. Then they read a Scripture passage and pray. The whole thing takes less than twenty minutes, and it's actually enjoyable.

"How often are we going to do this?" Casey asks.

"Once a week."

"Can't we do it more often?"

○ Talk about It

- What is your experience with family devotions?
- What factors prevent families from getting together to talk about their lives and about what God says in his Word?
- What, in your opinion, is the value of family devotions?
- What are your biggest fears and hopes about beginning a family devotional time?

☑ Check It Out

Read Deuteronomy 6:4-9 and discuss how this passage relates to family devotions.

♡ Apply It

This passage in Deuteronomy sets a pattern that helps us relate the Word of God to our daily lives. We are to love God, think constantly about his commandments, teach his commandments to our children, and live each day by the guidelines in his Word. God emphasized the importance of parents' teaching the Bible to their children. The church and Christian schools cannot be used to escape from this responsibility. The Bible provides so many opportunities for object lessons and practical teaching that it would be a shame to study it only in church on Sundays. Eternal truths are most effectively learned in the loving environment of a God-fearing home.

♟ Tip for Parents

Don't get too heavy with family devotions. Make them brief and fun. It is far better to spend ten minutes on a regular basis, than to pour it on strong for an hour and bore your kids out of their skulls. Most parents have found that the more low key and spontaneous they are about family devotions, the more receptive their children will be.

Discipline

Derek and Tucker are riding their bikes one afternoon when Derek suggests, "Hey, let's have a plum war!"

"A what?"

"A plum war. You get on that side of the Suttons' yard under that plum tree, and I'll stay over here by this one. Then we try to hit each other. The first one to get five hits wins."

Tucker isn't sure. "I don't know. Maybe the Suttons want to eat those plums. Besides, they're not home."

"Of course they're not home! You think we'd do it if they were? I think you're chicken. You're just scared I'm going nail you in the head with an old rotten plum!"

The challenge is too much for Tucker. Within thirty seconds the boys have jumped the fence and are frantically hurling plums at each other. In all the excitement, Derek fails to note that many of his misses are sailing into the Suttons' carport. Twenty minutes later, with the score three hits to two in favor of Tucker, the boys run out of ammunition and call it a day.

When Tucker gets home three hours later, his mom marches him up the street to apologize to Mr. Sutton, clean up the mess, and offer to pay for the damage. When he gets home from that, he finds out he is grounded for three weeks.

And Derek? No punishment at all, just a warning to "stay away from that old grouch, Mr. Sutton."

Tucker can't believe he's getting punished and Derek gets off scot-free!

○ Talk about It

- Should Tucker and Derek have gotten in trouble for what they did? Why or why not?
- What is the purpose of discipline/correction?
- Was Tucker's punishment appropriate for what he did?
- What is the most effective kind of discipline/correction? Why?

☑ Check It Out

Read Proverbs 3:11-12; 13:24; and 29:15, 17 for some important insights into the value of discipline.

♡ Apply It

It is not easy for a loving parent to discipline a child, but it is necessary. The greatest responsibility that God gives parents is the nurture and guidance of their children. Disciplining children averts long-range disaster. Without correction, children grow up with no clear understanding of right and wrong and with little direction to their lives. Lack of discipline puts parents' love in question because it shows a lack of concern for the character development of their children. Don't be afraid to discipline your children. It is an act of love. Remember, however, that your efforts cannot make your children wise; they can only encourage your children to seek God's wisdom above all else!

Tip for Parents

In a non-heated moment, share with your child(ren) about your own childhood experiences of being disciplined. Make sure they understand that the goal of discipline is not punitive but corrective. (You may wish to read Hebrews 12 to help them see that the motive behind biblical discipline is love.)

Dishonesty

Kimberly Walters is cooking dinner, glancing through the day's mail, and doing some last-minute preparation before her women's Bible study when the phone rings.

Her husband, Steven, answers the phone and announces, "Honey, it's Carla."

Kimberly rolls her eyes, gets a disgusted look on her face, and whispers, "If I get on the phone with her, I'll be stuck for thirty minutes! Tell her I can't come to the phone right now."

"You want me to lie to her?"

"I didn't say that. Look, I'll step in the bathroom for a minute. Tell her that. Tell her I'll have to call her back." With that, Kimberly disappears down the hallway.

Steven shakes his head but delivers the message to his talkative neighbor.

When he hangs up, eight-year-old Angelle looks up from her homework and says, "Dad, was that telling the truth?"

Steven feels a wave of conviction wash over him, but he decides to play dumb. "What do you mean, sweetheart?"

"I mean Mom acted like she couldn't talk on the phone. But it seemed more like she didn't want to."

Just then Kimberly walks back into the kitchen. Steven decides to pass the buck. "Tell you what, Angelle, why don't you ask your Mom the same question you asked me."

○ Talk about It

- Have you ever been in a situation like the one the Walters faced? What did you do?
- If Kimberly actually went to the bathroom, was her excuse for not talking to Carla a lie?
- What, if anything, is the difference between a lie and a "little white lie"?
- What happens when we get caught in a lie?

☑ Check It Out

Read Proverbs 12:13, 17, 19, and 22 and apply these verses to the situation just described.

♡ Apply It

Sinful talk is twisting the facts to support your claims. Those who do this are likely to be trapped by their own lies. But for someone who always tells the truth, the facts—plain and unvarnished—can always be trusted. Truth is always timely; it applies today and in the future. Because it is connected with God's changeless character, it must also be seen in the lives of his children.

♟ Tip for Parents

Remember that your children are far more influenced by what you do than by what you say. If your children catch you "shading the truth," immediately admit your wrong, and take quick steps to make amends.

Divorce

At dinner ten-year-old Meredith casually asks, "Why do people get divorced?"

Mrs. King passes the salt and pepper to her husband, gives him a quick glance, and replies, "Why do you ask?"

"Because Shelby told me today that her mom and dad were getting divorced and that her dad is moving back to the East Coast."

Mr. King grimaces and shakes his head. "I can't believe that. That's terrible!"

Mrs. King is watching Meredith closely. "Did Shelby seem upset?"

"Not really. She said it was probably better. She said her mom and dad argued all the time."

"I'm so sorry to hear that."

There is a long pause.

"Well, you still didn't answer my question. Why do people get divorced?"

Mr. King clears his throat. "Meredith, that's a tough question to answer. But, basically, to have the kind of marriage that God wants you to have, you have to be forgiving and unselfish. You have to talk to each other and share your feelings. And when you have arguments, you have to work really hard to resolve them."

"What if you fall out of love?"

"What do you mean?"

"Well, that's what Shelby said happened to her parents. She said they fell out of love with each other."

"Meredith, love isn't a feeling. I mean, it often comes with feelings. But ultimately love is a commitment. Your dad and I got married twelve years ago. We stood in front of God and our families and friends, and we promised to stay together for the rest of our lives. When you love somebody, you stick with them through the bad times as well as the good."

"So you and Dad aren't going to get divorced?"

"Nope. Whatever hard times might come, we will get through them with God's help." "That's right, honey," Mr. King adds, reaching out and squeezing his wife's hand.

☯ Talk about It

- Who do you know who's gotten divorced?
- Why do you think people divorce?
- What are some ways men, women, boys, and girls are affected by divorce?
- What are the dangers of building a marriage based solely on "feelings of love"?
- What factors can lessen a couple's likelihood of divorce?

☑ Check It Out

Read Matthew 19:1-9 to find out what Jesus taught about divorce.

♡ Apply It

Jesus' first word about divorce upheld the sanctity of marriage. Before considering the qualifications and conditions that may necessitate or permit divorce, Jesus pointed to an overriding divine plan for stable, long-term, monogamous marriage. Marriage is a gift from God, designed by him to be a committed partnership between a man and a woman. So strong is the bond that the two persons in it should be regarded as if they are one. Divorces will happen—they are the result of a good plan gone rotten because of greed, lust, and selfishness. But despite all that, marriage is good, strong, and endurable. That was God's intention and design.

♛ Tip for Parents

Commitment is fast becoming a meaningless word in our society. People base commitments on fickle feelings and deceptive desires. Look for teachable moments in everyday life (caring for a pet, finishing a project, etc.) in which you can model and teach this truth.

Encouragement

It was a fairly typical morning in the Brandon household: scrambling to eat breakfast and get lunches together, trying to decide what to wear, gathering books and notebooks, making beds and putting dirty clothes in the laundry hamper, and standing in line to use the rest room.

Listen to some of the comments that were made and exchanges that took place. See how the Brandon family compares to your own.

"You're such a pig! Why do you always eat all the waffles?!"

"Mom! I told you I wanted turkey, not ham. How come you don't listen to me?"

"I have nothing to wear! Look at this; I look like a homeless person."

"I am sick and tired of you leaving your room looking like a tornado just passed through it. If you are going to live like a hog, maybe we should start treating you like one."

"Get out of the bathroom! You've been in there for at least an hour! And it wouldn't matter if you stood there looking in the mirror for *ten* hours, you'd still have that goofy haircut!"

⟳ Talk about It

- If someone had secretly taped your family's interaction yesterday (or this morning), what comments would he or she have heard?
- Would you describe the conversation in your home as mostly positive or mostly negative?
- What is encouragement and how might the conversations above have been different if each member of the Brandon family had made it a goal to encourage others?
- How can you encourage someone in your family today or tomorrow?

✉ Check It Out

Read Romans 12:9-18 for a look at how we ought to treat one another.

♡ Apply It

As you near the end of a long race, your legs ache, your throat burns, and your whole body cries out for you to stop. This is when family and friends are most valuable. Their encouragement helps you push through the pain to the finish line. In the same way, Christians are to encourage one another. A word of encouragement offered at the right moment can be the difference between finishing well and collapsing along the way. Look around you—in your family and among your friends. Be sensitive to others' need for encouragement, and offer supportive words or actions.

♟ Tip for Parents

Our world beats us down all the time. Make your home a place where people are built up and encouraged. Try this exercise: Have your family sit in a circle on the floor. One at a time, put each family member in the center of the circle. Then have everyone share one thing they really admire or appreciate about the person inside the ring. Stress character qualities over appearance, clothing, etc. Done correctly, this affirmation game makes everyone feel wonderful!

Envy

Every time LaShawn is around Eldred, he gets mad. Eldred has *everything* going for him.

Eldred is the biggest, fastest kid in the neighborhood. Nobody can catch him in football, and nobody can guard him in basketball.

Eldred is also the smartest kid at school. All the teachers love him, and all the women at church love him.

On top of that, Eldred has the coolest looking bike around. It had to cost at least two hundred dollars, maybe even more. He won it in an essay contest.

And if all that weren't enough, Eldred has a really close relationship with his dad. In fact, his dad takes him fishing at least once a week. And this summer, according to Eldred, his whole family is going to visit the Grand Canyon.

Just thinking about Eldred makes LaShawn upset.

○ Talk about It

- What is envy?
- How is envy different from jealousy?
- Why is envy a dangerous thing?
- How are resentment and discontentment related to envy?
- What are some things or qualities you don't have but wish you did?
- What should a person do if he or she realizes he or she is being envious of someone else?

☑ Check It Out

Consider these Scriptures that address the sin of jealousy—Proverbs 14:30; 1 Corinthians 13:4; and Galatians 5:26.

♡ Apply It

The tenth commandment tells us not to covet (Exodus 20:17). To covet is to wish to have the possessions of others. It goes beyond simply admiring someone else's possessions or thinking *I'd like to have one of those.* Coveting includes envy—resenting the fact that others have what you don't. It destroys what little enjoyment we get out of the possessions we already have. Since only God can supply all our needs, true contentment is found only in him. When you begin to covet, try to determine if a more basic need is leading you to envy. For example, you may covet someone's success, not because you want to take it away from him, but because you would like to feel as appreciated by others as he is. If that is the case, pray that God will help you deal with your resentment and meet your basic needs.

♟ Tip for Parents

Parents can help minimize the power of envy by emphasizing the unique gifts and talents of each child. Resist the common tendency to compare your offspring to each other. Refuse the temptation to say, "Why can't you be more like your brother (or sister)?" These kinds of actions only fan the flames of envy and fuel the fires of resentment. Pray that your children will come to appreciate their one-of-a-kind personality and potential.

Escape

It's been about a year since David Hoover died suddenly at the age of forty.

Counselors told family members that after an initial period of shock and denial, they could expect to feel great anger and despair. "That's a natural part of the grieving process," they said.

But have the surviving Hoovers handled their grief appropriately? Consider:

David's wife, Kate, has been taking tranquilizers on a regular basis. "I just can't sleep if I don't!" she says.

Daughter Emily seems to be glued to the television. You can almost always find her with the remote in hand. Or else she's watching another video. (Some weekends she watches as many as six movies!)

Son Daniel has poured himself into basketball. That's about all he does from the time he gets home from school until dark.

⟳ Talk about It

- Are the actions of the members of the Hoover family normal, or do they strike you as unhealthy? Why?
- What's the difference between relaxing and escaping? between enjoying a hobby and escaping?
- Is it wrong to "veg out" or escape? Why or why not?
- Our word *amusement* literally means "without thinking." If that is the case, is amusement always a healthy activity? Why or why not?
- When you don't want to face the world around you, what methods of escaping do you tend to employ? Why?
- What are the alternatives to running away from tough problems?

✉ Check It Out

Rather than running away to try to find satisfaction, God wants us to come to him for deep fulfillment (see Isaiah 55:1-2 and Matthew 11:28-30).

♡ Apply It

Jesus said that the yoke he places on us is easy (Matthew 11:28-30). A yoke is a heavy wooden harness that fits over the shoulders of an ox or oxen. It is attached to a piece of equipment the oxen are to pull. A person may be carrying heavy burdens of grief, sin, worry, excessive demands of religious leaders (Matthew 23:4; Acts 15:10), oppression and persecution, or weariness in the search for God.

Jesus frees us from all these burdens. The rest he promises is love, healing, and peace with God, not the end of all hardship. A relationship with God changes meaningless, wearisome toil into spiritual productivity and purpose.

Tip for Parents

In his insightful book *Finding God,* Larry Crabb makes a compelling argument for the idea that God's desire and plan for our lives is not to make us feel better, but to help us find God. Though it often goes against our nature to pursue God in the midst of great pain, this is precisely what we must do. Our children need to understand that though escaping or running away from our problems may temporarily ease our pain, it is not a real solution.

Evangelism

Last Saturday a man came to First Church to lead a special seminar called "Telling the Good News." Over forty church members, including the whole Malone family, attended. The speaker was both funny and inspiring as he trained people to communicate their faith in Christ more effectively. At the end of the day, participants were challenged to begin praying for opportunities to talk about the Lord.

On Monday at breakfast the Malones did just that. They asked God to give them chances to express their faith, the courage to do so, and the ability to explain the gospel clearly.

Here's what happened to Mitchell after school that very day: In the parking lot, he watched a girl accidentally back into a new pickup truck. Jumping out of her car, she immediately burst into tears. Nobody else was around, so Mitchell went over to see if he could help. And as he did, suddenly the thought ran through his mind: *Maybe* this *is a good chance to share my faith.*

Mitchell began to talk about Jesus. At first the girl listened politely, but then she looked at him strangely and said, "Hey, look, if you want to help me, that's great. But I really don't need a sermon right now!"

○ Talk about It

- Talk about a time when you tried to talk about Jesus to someone. What happened?
- Why do so many Christians feel uncomfortable talking about their faith?
- How should sensitivity play a part in our attempts to witness?
- If Mitchell came to you and told you about his failed attempt at evangelism, what would you tell him?
- What people—friends, neighbors, classmates, coworkers, family members—do you know who need to meet Christ in a personal way?

☑ Check It Out

Consider the way Jesus talked about spiritual matters with a woman he met one day near Jacob's well—John 4:1-42.

♡ Apply It

When we tell others about Christ, it is important to always be gracious in what we say (Colossians 4:6). No matter how much sense the message makes, delivering it in a crude or discourteous way cancels out its effectiveness. Just as we like to be respected, we must respect others if we want them to listen to what we say.

👥 Tip for Parents

Joseph Aldrich has written a terrific book on lifestyle evangelism entitled *Gentle Persuasion.* If your children are age ten or older, this would be a great resource for the whole family to read and discuss together.

Evolution

While watching a nature show on public television, the Henriksen family hears the narrator make statements and utter phrases like:

"We can now know much more about our prehuman ancestors. . . .

". . . the scientific fact of evolution . . .

"Like other animals, man is driven by his will to survive. . . .

"It is tragic when uninformed individuals put more credence in faith than in the irrefutable facts of science. . . ."

Mr. Henriksen finally grabs the remote control and changes channels.

"Dad, why'd you do that? They were just about to show that crocodile eating a deer."

"Son, I am sick and tired of hearing that evolution junk! They find one or two toe bones in the desert somewhere, let their imaginations run wild, and before you know it, they've 'recreated' a complete history of some fictitious ape-man. They even tell you what it ate for lunch! It's atheism disguised as science."

"But, Dad, they weren't saying anything on that show that they don't teach us at school."

"I know, Byron. Look, I was never much of a science student. I don't know all the facts to show exactly where the theory of evolution is weak, but I do know that a number of the leading scientists in the world are having second thoughts about Darwin and his whole evolutionary scheme. A number of books have been published about—"

"Dad," the Henriksens' twelve-year-old daughter interrupts, "if you're worried that Byron and I are going to start believing in evolution, you can relax. When the teacher gets off on that stuff, my friends and I just look at each other and roll our eyes."

⟲ Talk about It

- What do you know about the evolution/Creation debate?
- Why is this topic so important?
- What do your teachers and friends believe about this issue?
- If we could find some good material on origins, would you like to do a "family study" to become more informed?

☑ Check It Out

Read Genesis 1:1-31 for the biblical view of the origin of the universe.

♡ Apply It

The creation story teaches us much about God and ourselves. First, we learn about God: (1) He is creative; (2) as the Creator he is distinct from his creation; and (3) he is eternal and in control of the world. We also learn about ourselves: (1) Since God chose to create us, we are valuable in his eyes; and (2) we are more important than the animals.

Tip for Parents

The Institute for Creation Research has a number of fine educational resources for children defending the biblical view of origins. If you would like a list of videos, books, magazines, or devotionals, write to them at:

Institute for Creation Research
P. O. Box 2667
El Cajon, CA 92021
(619) 448-0900

Excellence

Take a peek at the actions of the Goldblums this weekend:

- When her mom asked her to clean up her room, Marla basically raked everything that was on the floor into a huge heap in the closet. Then she shoved everything else into her mostly empty desk drawers. "OK, Mom!" she announced. "I cleaned my room!"
- Mark had soccer practice. Since he stayed up late the night before, he didn't feel like practicing. While everybody else was hustling, Mark was dogging it.
- Mrs. Goldblum waited until Sunday morning to throw together her Sunday school lesson for the fourth-grade girls.
- Mr. Goldblum skipped out of a highly recommended Saturday-morning seminar on fathering (one about which he's been saying for weeks, "I definitely need to go to that!"). Instead, he spent four hours cleaning his boat.

⟳ Talk about It

- What does it mean to be excellent?
- Look up *mediocre* or *mediocrity* in the dictionary. Discuss the definitions. Give some examples of things that are mediocre.
- In what ways did the Goldblums fail to demonstrate excellence?
- What are some areas in which you are currently excelling?
- What are some activities in which you need to make more of an effort to do your best?
- What does it mean to be excellent in the Christian life?

☑ Check It Out

Consider the apostle Paul's exhortations to be excellent—1 Corinthians 9:24 and 2 Timothy 2:15.

♡ Apply It

Living the Christian life is like running a race (1 Corinthians 9:24-27), and winning a race requires purpose and discipline. Living for Christ, in other words, takes hard work, self-denial, and grueling preparation. As Christians, we are running toward our heavenly reward. The essential disciplines of prayer, Bible study, and worship equip us to run with vigor and stamina. Don't merely observe from the grandstand; don't just turn out to jog a couple of laps each morning. Train diligently—your spiritual progress depends upon it.

▮▮ Tip for Parents

In a culture where the prevailing attitudes are "do just enough to get by" and "take the path of least resistance," we have to work overtime to instill in our children the biblical value of pursuing excellence. Remind your kids (and model for them the truth) that everything we attempt is to be done for the Lord himself (1 Corinthians 10:31). Make that your own goal in life—to bring God glory in every act, even the insignificant ones.

Faith

"Dad, is our religion the right one?"

"Well, it's biblical, if that's what you mean."

"So are the other religions wrong?"

"Why are you asking these questions?"

"I dunno. I guess because in my class we've got people who believe in all kinds of stuff."

"Like what?"

"Well, Rashid and his family are Muslims. And so they believe in Muhammed. And then Kris is Mormon. And Joel is Jewish. And I think Amy's grandfather is a Buddhist, but I'm not sure if Amy is."

"That's a lot of different beliefs."

"Yeah, and anyway, we got in an argument. I told 'em they were wrong if they didn't believe the Bible."

"What did they say?"

"That they have just as much faith as I do."

○ Talk about It

- Should Christians argue about religious/spiritual matters? Why or why not?
- What's more important—having faith or having faith in the right thing?
- Is it possible to be sincere but to also be sincerely wrong? Give an example.
- What would you say to someone who accused Christianity of being "too narrow"?
- How can we know if our faith is built on truth?
- What religion or faith would you like to know more about?

☑ Check It Out

Notice that Paul declared that true faith must be "in our Lord Jesus" (Acts 20:21). Notice also that Jesus said he is the only way to God (John 14:6).

♡ Apply It

Some people think that to say Jesus is the only way (John 14:6) is much too narrow-minded. In reality, the way is wide enough for the whole world if the world chooses to accept it. As the *way,* Jesus is our path to the Father. As the *truth,* he is the reality of all God's promises. As the *life,* he joins his divine life to ours, both now and eternally. Instead of worrying about how limited it sounds to have only one way, we should say, "Thank you, God, for providing a sure way to get to you!"

♦♦ Tip for Parents

Pick up a book that compares and contrasts the world's major religions. (Your pastor or local Christian bookstore can recommend some good titles.) Such a volume is a wonderful resource and teaching tool when your children encounter situations like the one described above.

Fashion

"Dawn, get down here now, or you're going to miss the bus!"

"All right, Mom! I said I'm coming!"

Twelve-year-old Dawn stares at herself in the bathroom mirror one final time. A big solitary tear trickles down her left cheek. Quickly she wipes it away with her sleeve.

Grabbing her backpack, Dawn runs down the stairs. As she makes her way out the front door and down the street to the bus stop, a hundred different thoughts whirl through her head—thoughts like these: *I look so stupid.... Why do I have to be the only one at school who wears these no-name clothes?... If Amanda Tucker teases me today about the way I look, I'm gonna slap her—or at least tell her off!... Why can't Mom let me get at least one pair of designer jeans?... Maybe I should do what Katherine does—get some makeup, put it on after I leave the house, and then take it off before Mom sees me.... I can't wait to be old enough to get a job. I'm going to work at the mall in a clothing store, and I'm gonna spend all my money on clothes!*

Sure enough, when Dawn gets to school, she bumps into Amanda in the hall between classes. "Nice dress, Dawn. You must have hit the garage sales this weekend."

Dawn doesn't slap her tormentor. And she doesn't yell. She just turns bright red and runs away.

⟳ Talk about It

- What is your favorite way to dress/favorite outfit? Why?
- How much emphasis do your friends at school or the office or church put on fashion and appearance?
- Some people argue that designer clothes are no better than basic brands but that we are paying for the "label." Do you agree? Why or why not? What makes people so obsessed with labels?

☑ Check It Out

Read 1 Peter 3:3-4. Though this passage is written to females, it teaches broad principles about fashion and appearance.

♡ Apply It

Imagine a mirror that could reflect what your character or soul looks like. What would be revealed if you stood in front of such a mirror? What is one thing you could do today to work on your "inner" appearance? Will you do it?

▮▮ Tip for Parents

Be sensitive to your children's natural tendency to want to fit in. Try to recall your own youthful quest for "fashion acceptance." For fun, pull out some old pictures and show them to your kids. They will no doubt get quite a laugh out of the silly hairstyles and outdated clothes. But they may also get to glimpse a crucial truth—that hot, to-die-for fashions never last and will one day seem ridiculous.

Favoritism

Eight-year-old Ellen Sibley jumps up and runs to the living room window (for the sixth time in the last half hour).

"Mom, when are they gonna get here?" she whines as she peers through the drapes. (This is at least the tenth time she has posed that question!)

Laura Sibley tries to be pleasant. "Sweetheart, I don't know. All they said was after lunch. They'll get here when they get here."

"But I want them to hurry. I want to start playing my new piano."

"I know you do, sweetie. And you'll get to tonight, I promise."

Ten-year-old Michael slides off his bar stool, gives his sister a dirty look, and mumbles, "I don't see what the big deal is. It's just a dumb ole piano." With that he marches down the hall toward his bedroom.

Laura assumes Michael is angry about not being allowed to eat an ice-cream sandwich. She's wrong.

Back in his bedroom, lying on the bed and staring at the ceiling, Michael is wondering why his parents will spend more than a thousand dollars on a piano for his sister—and it's not her birthday, and it's not Christmas. *They won't let me have a bike that costs a measly two hundred dollars, but they'll buy her a piano no matter how much it costs! They won't let me take karate lessons, but they let her take piano lessons. No matter what, she always ends up getting whatever she wants. And I get nothing. It's not fair!*

○ Talk about It

- Are parents obligated to spend exactly the same amount of money on each of their children? Why or why not?
- What are the dangers of favoritism in a family?
- What advice would you give Michael in the story above?
- How would it change your opinion of this situation if you knew that Michael didn't get a bike but he did get his own computer?

☑ Check It Out

Read Genesis 37:3-4 for an example of what happens in a family when parents show favoritism to one child.

♡ Apply It

In Joseph's day, everyone had a robe or cloak. Robes were used to warm oneself, to bundle up belongings for a trip, to wrap babies, to sit on, or even to serve as security for a loan. Most robes were knee length, short sleeved, and plain. In contrast, Joseph's robe was probably of the kind worn by royalty—long sleeved, ankle length, and colorful. The robe became a symbol of Jacob's favoritism toward Joseph, and it aggravated the already strained relations between Joseph and his brothers. Favoritism in families may be unavoidable, but its divisive effects should be minimized. Parents may not be able to change their feelings toward a favorite child, but they can change their actions toward the others.

♙♙ Tip for Parents

Rather than focusing on the amount of money you are spending per child, focus on helping each child develop his or her gifts and abilities. Be aware of inequities (real or imagined) that your children perceive, and encourage them to talk with you about how they feel. Try to listen and understand their feelings without becoming defensive. There will always be times when kids think their brother or sister has it better than they do, but make sure that fundamentally your kids know they're equally loved and valued.

Fear

Everyone in Randall Estates is talking about the events of Saturday night. Someone poisoned the Collins family's German shepherd and then broke into their home. Not only did the criminals steal items valued at more than eight thousand dollars, but they also scrawled threats on one of the bathroom mirrors using a tube of lipstick.

At dinner the Novak family is discussing the burglary.

Fourteen-year-old Brad is insistent. "Dad, I think we should get an alarm system. We could do it this Saturday. They don't cost that much—about two or three hundred bucks—if you buy one at the home-improvement center and do it yourself. Patricia's dad put one in their house last summer. He said it was easy."

"I'd like to do that, Son, but the truth is that we can't afford even a low-cost system. The best we can probably do right now is add a couple of spotlights out back. And I talked to Mr. Batt and Mrs. Vignery about getting the neighborhood watch program going again. We've got good locks on all the windows and deadbolts on all the doors. Humanly speaking, I'd say we've done about all we can do."

"Are those men gonna come to our house?" whispers nine-year-old Fran. She looks terrified.

○ Talk about It

- Do you know anyone whose home has been burglarized? How did you feel when you heard about it?
- What are your biggest fears? Why?
- When you do feel afraid, how do you overcome those fearful feelings?
- How do news reports of violence and tragedy contribute to our tendency to be afraid?

☑ Check It Out

Read Isaiah 41:10 and comment on how it applies to the situations that make you afraid.

♡ Apply It

Fear is a dark shadow that envelops us and ultimately imprisons us within ourselves. Each of us has been a prisoner of fear at one time or another— fear of rejection, misunderstanding, uncertainty, sickness, or even death. But we can conquer fear by using the bright, liberating light of the Lord who brings salvation. If we want to dispel the darkness of fear, let us remember that God is always with us.

♛♛ Tip for Parents

Don't make light of your child's fears. They may seem irrational to you, but they are very real to the one who feels them. Hugs and reassurances can help. Meanwhile, take comfort in the fact that childhood anxieties typically disappear in a short time.

Feelings

This morning when James Anders woke up, he didn't *feel* like going to work. He would have preferred to roll over and go back to sleep or go fishing or even do yard work—anything but go into the office. Nevertheless, in spite of his *feelings,* he had to go anyway.

When Tricia Anders told her son Mark to clean his room, he replied, "I'll do it later. I don't *feel* like doing it right now."

"No," his mom replied, "you'll do it right now."

"Mom, didn't you hear me? I said I don't *feel* like it."

"I heard you. And I really don't care too much how you *feel* about it. That's not the issue. It needs to be done, and I want you to do it."

Now, at the end of the day, James and Tricia are exhausted. They both keep looking at the clock. In a few minutes they need to be leaving for their fellowship group. "You *feel* like going?" James asks.

"Not really," Tricia replies.

⟳ Talk about It

- Why are our feelings so inconsistent from day to day or even from hour to hour?
- What determines whether we feel eager to do something or not?
- How much of a factor should our feelings be in making decisions?
- What are some things you have to do regardless of how you feel?

☑ Check It Out

Consider that the following passages (like the overwhelming majority in the Bible) say nothing about feelings. They simply describe or call for doing God's will, period: Genesis 6:22; Ephesians 5:22, 25; 6:1-4.

♡ Apply It

Ezekiel didn't feel like obeying God, either (Ezekiel 3:14-15). Soon after God appointed him to preach to the people of Israel, he felt bitter and angry. The sins and negative attitudes of the people had put him in no mood to become a prophet. Still, he had to begin the tedious job of prophesying among his people, no matter how little they cared about God's messages. Ezekiel remembered the vision of the living creatures and the rumbling wheels. He remembered that he had nothing to fear because God was with him. Despite knowing the probable outcome, Ezekiel obeyed God.

Times of great joy when we feel close to God will be followed by times of great blahness. Sins, struggles, and everyday responsibilities will overwhelm us. Like Ezekiel, we need to obey God even when we don't feel like it. Don't let feelings hinder your obedience.

⫙ Tip for Parents

In our experiential culture, feelings are king! The battle cry of the late sixties "If it feels good, do it!" (together with its unstated counterpart "If it doesn't feel good, don't do it!") is still very much a part of our collective mind-set. Teach your children at an early age that feelings ultimately don't matter. Far more important are the values of responsibility and commitment.

For real shock value, don't cook one night or do anything else that is nice and helpful. When your kids complain (and they will!), tell them you just didn't *feel* like being a mom and/or dad. Done with the right spirit, this little exercise can bring about a powerful teachable moment.

Foolishness

Listen to what happened to Rebecca over the weekend.

First, she ignored what her parents told her about staying home and doing her homework. Instead, when they left for a trip to the mall, she went down the street to a friend's house.

When her parents got back and said, "Where were you? We tried to call, and no one answered," Rebecca lied, "Oh, I guess the ringer must have gotten turned off."

When her parents did a little investigating, Rebecca's scheme began to unravel. Immediately she got defensive. Angrily she raised her voice and smarted off to her parents.

When Rebecca's parents grounded her for two weeks and tried to explain why they were doing so, Rebecca tuned them out. In her mind she was thinking, *They're so stupid. I can't wait until I turn eighteen!*

⟳ Talk about It

- What do you think about the situation you just read about? What's Rebecca's deal? Why is she so angry?
- What is a fool?
- What are the consequences for acting foolish? Can you think of someone who did something foolish and who got into big trouble? What happened?
- What are some things you have done in your life that are foolish?
- Why do parents and children clash so much?
- How can you keep from acting foolish this week?

☑ Check It Out

The book of Proverbs is like a checklist for spotting foolish behavior—Proverbs 10:23; 12:16; 14:16; 15:5; 18:2; and 28:26.

♡ Apply It

Proverbs 9 portrays Wisdom and Folly (foolishness) as rival young women, each preparing a feast and inviting people to it. But Wisdom is a responsible woman of character, while Folly is a prostitute serving stolen food. Wisdom appeals first to the mind, Folly to the senses. It is easier to excite the senses, but the pleasures of Folly do not last. By contrast, the satisfaction that wisdom brings lasts forever.

♟ Tip for Parents

Often the root cause of foolishness is pride. Thus it is not just kids who can be foolish. Parents are susceptible, too. Make sure you are not foolish in your child rearing. Humbly seek the counsel of parents who are a bit farther down the road. One great resource is *Parenting Passages* by David Veerman. That book offers the insights needed to navigate through the various stages of life.

Forgiveness

Rob and his friends come bursting through the kitchen door after a big game of football. They are sweaty and thirsty but still have energy to burn.

"Can you guys believe that catch I made for the winning touchdown?" Brad brags.

Britt laughs. "The guy covering you fell down!"

"And you're twice as fast as him!" Rob adds.

"Yeah, but he tipped the ball, and I had to dive backwards. And I still caught it with one hand!"

"You were lucky!"

"No way. It was skill. I'm like Jerry Rice. Watch, I'll show you. Throw it low and hard." Brad starts jogging across the living room, and so Rob fires the ball at him.

Crash!

The ball hits a ceramic cat sitting on top of the TV and shatters it against the wall.

Rob's sister, Amy, comes running into the room. "What was that?!" she yelps. Then she spies the shards of glass on the floor.

Rob immediately begins apologizing. "Amy, I'm sorry. It was an accident. I didn't mean to. I'll get you another one."

Amy is furious. "You can't get me another one! They don't make 'em anymore! That cat was a gift from Grandma! It was about fifty years old! You guys are really gonna get it!" Amy storms out of the room to find her mom.

○ Talk about It

- Who needs to be forgiven in this story?
- Why is it so difficult to forgive those who have wronged us?
- How does it feel to be forgiven?
- How would you define forgiveness?
- Have you done something to a family member for which you need to ask forgiveness?

☑ Check It Out

Read Matthew 18:21-35.

♡ Apply It

The rabbis taught that people should forgive those who offend them—but only three times. Peter, trying to be especially generous, asked Jesus if seven (the "perfect" number) was enough times to forgive someone. But Jesus answered, "Seventy times seven," meaning that we shouldn't even keep track of how many times we forgive someone. Because God has forgiven all our sins, we should not withhold forgiveness from others. We should always forgive those who are truly repentant, no matter how many times they ask.

♟ Tip for Parents

Forgiveness is not denying that one has been wronged. It is not rationalizing or explaining away the sin of another person. Nor is forgiveness "forgetting" in the sense of having amnesia about a prior offense. It is the conscious decision to cancel a debt that is owed by another. Make sure you clarify these issues in explaining the concept of forgiveness to your children.

Freedom

Lindsay, fourteen, is in her bedroom crying. She's not only sad, she's mad. Why? Her parents won't let her go to a friend's party. Their reason? They don't think it will have enough adult supervision. And furthermore, they have some concerns about some of the kids who will be there.

It's not fair! Lindsay thinks to herself as she covers her face with a pillow. *They treat me like a little kid. They hover over me and monitor every little thing I do. I'm like a prisoner in my own family!* The frustration Lindsay feels inside wells up until she can't stand it any longer. "Aaaargh!" she finally screams into the pillow.

Rolling over, she looks up and then out the window. She begins pondering her future. *I can't wait to graduate and go off to college and get away from all these stupid rules.* Just thinking about the prospect causes Lindsay to smile. *Hmmm. Three and a half years. Then I'll be able to do whatever I want. If I want to drink, I can. I'll be able to stay out all night, go to any party, pick my own friends, date anybody I please.*

Suddenly Lindsay is talking out loud. "That's all I want—my freedom. To be able to do anything I want. No restrictions."

○ Talk about It

- Have you ever felt like Lindsay? When? What happened?
- Why do you think parents set up so many rules?
- Are rules necessarily a bad thing? Explain.
- What do you think about Lindsay's definition of freedom? Is it a good one? Why or why not?
- In what ways is the chance to do whatever you want actually *not* real freedom at all?
- What would you tell Lindsay if she came to you for advice?

✉ Check It Out

The desire to be free from rules is not new. Read what happened to the first man and woman in Genesis 3:1-6.

♡ Apply It

When they first sinned, Adam and Eve got exactly what they wanted: an intimate knowledge of both good and evil (Genesis 3:5). But they got it by doing evil, and the results were disastrous. Sometimes we have the illusion that freedom means getting to do anything we want. But God says that the best kind of freedom—freedom without fear or risk—comes from obedience and knowing what *not* to do. The restrictions he gives us are for our good, to help us avoid evil. We have the freedom to walk in front of a speeding car, but we don't need to be hit to realize it would be foolish to do so. Don't listen to Satan's temptations. You don't have to do evil to gain more experience and learn more about life.

♟ Tip for Parents

When you establish rules for your children, take the time to explain the reason behind each regulation. Your kids will still struggle with submitting (that's human nature), but at least they will know that your boundaries are not arbitrary. Emphasize your intent to protect (from harm) and to provide (fulfillment in life).

Friendship

A new family recently moved into the neighborhood. They're the Allens from California, and they have four children, ages seven to fifteen.

Susie Flanagan is concerned about the impact two of the new boys seem to be having on her thirteen-year-old son, Sean.

Ronnie, Ricky, and Sean have been together almost daily all week. On Saturday they rode their bikes out to an old, abandoned fishing camp on the river. Sean didn't "technically" break any rules in going that far from home, but his behavior certainly wasn't very wise.

On Sunday morning Sean acted disinterested in church. As soon as Sunday lunch was over, Sean headed over to the Allens', where he stayed all afternoon.

Monday the boys got into trouble at the neighborhood pool. The lifeguard said they were making rude comments and disregarding her instructions. Sean downplayed the incident, saying it was all a big misunderstanding.

Tuesday Sean came home with a CD by some new heavy-metal group called Toxemia. Disappearing into his bedroom, he cranked up his stereo. Susie was in his room within sixty seconds. "Sean, what is that?" She practically had to shout over the high-pitched shrieks and wails.

"It's just a CD I borrowed from Ronnie."

"Well, I don't think I like that music. It sounds like a continuous plane crash."

Sean rolled his eyes. "Mom, they're really good if you listen to them."

"Well, turn it down about a hundred decibels."

As Susie walked back into the kitchen, she wondered what was happening to her son. In less than a week, he went from being a sweet, compliant son to a distant, angry adolescent.

○ Talk about It

- How much do friends affect the way we think, talk, and act?
- What kind of rules should families have about friends?
- What qualities should we look for in a friend?
- Who is your best friend and what makes that relationship so special?
- What five words would your best friend use to describe you?

☑ Check It Out

See the warning against associating with the wrong kinds of people in 1 Corinthians 15:33.

♡ Apply It

Our friends and associates can have a profound influence on us, often in very subtle ways. If we insist on friendships with those who mock what God considers important, we might sin by becoming indifferent to God's will. Don't let your relationships with unbelievers lead you away from Christ or cause your faith to waver. Do your friends build up your faith, or do they tear it down?

♟ Tip for Parents

As children move into adolescence, their friendships tend to become all-important and all-consuming. Parents who "make a huge deal" out of their kids' friendships sometimes do more harm than good. The most significant way you can influence your children in this area is to pray daily that they will choose friends wisely.

Gambling

The McKinneys are watching the evening news to see who won the big play-off game when a story comes on about the newest winner of the state lotto. She's a middle-aged waitress from a little place called Crestwood. After taxes she will get almost $17 million spread out over the next twenty years. She tells the reporter she'll use the money to help her grandkids go to college.

Mr. McKinney shakes his head and announces to no one in particular, "I'm telling you, this country has gone nuts over gambling! Lotteries, bingo parlors, casinos, horse racing, riverboat gambling—everybody wants to be an instant millionaire. Everybody wants something for nothing."

"Aw, Dad, what's so terrible about buying a lottery ticket every now and then? They only cost a dollar. Besides, most of the profits go to the public schools."

"It's wasting money, that's what. We're supposed to use our money wisely. We're supposed to 'lay up treasure in heaven.' Besides, the Bible talks about working hard, not chasing fantasies."

The McKinneys' fifteen-year-old son, Ray, quietly listens to his Dad's words and thinks to himself, *I don't get Dad. He condemns people who pay a dollar for a lottery ticket, but he gladly spends money for postage stamps to mail in those magazine sweepstakes entries. Isn't a mail-in sweepstakes basically the same thing as a lottery—just a little bit cheaper?*

♻ Talk about It

- What do you think about Ray's questions? Is a mail-in sweepstakes merely a "lottery for the price of a postage stamp"?
- Why do you think gambling is so popular in this country?
- If you unexpectedly received a large sum of money, what would you do with it and why?
- How can Christians avoid getting caught up in the "get rich quick" trap?

☑ Check It Out

Read 1 Timothy 6:7-10 for a closer look at how the desire for wealth can be dangerous.

♡ Apply It

Despite overwhelming evidence to the contrary, most people still believe that money brings happiness. Rich people craving greater riches can be caught in an endless cycle that only ends in ruin and destruction. How can you keep away from the love of money? Paul gives us some guidelines: (1) Realize that one day riches will all be gone (1 Timothy 6:7, 17); (2) be content with what you have (6:8); (3) monitor what you are willing to do to get more money (6:9, 10); (4) love people more than money (6:11); (5) love God's work more than money (6:11); and (6) freely share what you have with others (6:18).

♟ Tip for Parents

When we practice thankfulness, we model for our children the virtue of contentment.

Giving

For nine months, the Stanfords have been planning to buy a trampoline. The model they want costs around $450.00. Here's the creative plan they've been using to save up enough money: Every day the family members empty their change into a big pickle jar. Every Sunday night they roll up their coins and see how close they are to their goal. Last week the tally stood at $348.50.

But today at church the Stanfords heard about a family in the community whose trailer home burned to the ground last night. All their belongings are gone, and their insurance is inadequate. Church members were challenged to give whatever they can afford—food, clothing, even cash.

Tonight as the Stanfords sit around silently counting the money in their trampoline fund, each feels strange inside. It's hard to think about bouncing and laughing when you know there's a family right up the road who has just lost everything.

Ten-year-old Megan feels like she should say something, but she's afraid her family will get mad at her. *If we buy that trampoline now, I'll never be able to enjoy it,* she reasons.

Little does she know that her fellow family members are thinking the same thing!

⟳ Talk about It

- What is one item you wish your family could purchase? Why?
- Is it wrong to buy things like trampolines? Why or why not?
- What is something you would have an easy time giving away? Why?
- What is something you would have a hard time giving away? Why?

☑ Check It Out

Read the command of Christ in Acts 20:35.

♡ Apply It

The point of giving is not so much the amount we give, but why and how we give. God does not want gifts given grudgingly. Instead, he wants us to give out of dedication to Christ, love for fellow believers, and the joy of helping those in need, as well as the fact that it is simply the good and right thing to do. Consider these four principles of giving: (1) Your willingness to give cheerfully is more important than the amount you give; (2) you should strive to fulfill your financial commitments; (3) if you give to others in need, they will, in turn, help you when you are in need; and (4) you should give as a response to Christ, not for anything you can get out of it. How well does your giving measure up?

▮▮ Tip for Parents

Consider establishing an ongoing family program of giving to worthwhile causes. Perhaps the family can do fund-raisers together. Or each member can contribute part of his or her allowance or wages. Let the whole family function as a kind of "foundation" and choose the individuals and/or charities they would like to support.

God's Goodness

"If God is good, how come bad things happen?"

That's the question a lot of people in Cedarton are asking this weekend.

Shannon Wagner is wrestling with that question. Her parents are in the middle of a nasty separation. And despite her many prayers for them to get back together, it looks as though they will end up divorcing.

The Fields are wondering if God is good after getting the results of a medical test on Friday that confirmed the worst: Mr. Field has lung cancer.

Bart Wiley and his family are struggling to believe in the goodness of God after coming home from an out-of-town trip and finding their house burned to the ground. Everything was lost, including all their family keepsakes and heirlooms.

☉ Talk about It

- Someone has said that it is easy to believe that God is powerful or that he is wise, but that it is often difficult (especially when you see how evil the world is) to believe that God is truly good. Do you agree with that statement? Why or why not?
- When in your life have you ever doubted the goodness of God?
- How can a person regain a sense of hope that God is, in fact, a loving, good God?
- What would you tell the people in the scenarios described above if they came to you for some encouragement?
- In what way or ways do you think Satan caused Adam and Eve to have doubts about God's goodness?
- If you had to list five reasons you *know* God is good, what evidence would you cite?

✉ Check It Out

Read Psalm 145, a great hymn about the goodness of God.

♡ Apply It

The serpent in the Garden tempted Eve by getting her to doubt God's goodness (Genesis 3:1-6). He implied that God was strict, stingy, and self-ish for not wanting Eve to share his knowledge of good and evil. Satan made Eve forget all that God had given her and, instead, focus on the one thing she couldn't have. We fall into trouble, too, whenever we dwell on the few things we don't have rather than on the countless things God has given us. The next time you are feeling sorry for yourself and what you don't have, consider all you *do* have and thank God. Then your doubts won't lead you into sin.

♟ Tip for Parents

Help your children see that *good* does not always equal *pleasant* or *fun*. For instance, it is good for an athlete to get into shape, but that experience is seldom enjoyable. It is good for a surgeon to remove a tumor, but that operation is never pain-free. If our kids can understand that God truly seeks our best, that he has a long-range plan in effect, and that we won't understand everything until we get to heaven, maybe they will cling to the notion of God's goodness.

God's Power

". . . and thanks for this food, in Jesus' name, amen."

"Karin, didn't you forget something?"

"What?"

"You didn't pray for Grandpa."

"Mom, you saw how he acted the whole time he was here. You heard what he said when we asked him if he wanted to go to church with us. We've been praying for him ever since I can remember. But what good does it do? He's never gonna change!"

"That's true, Mom," eight-year old Brad chimed in. "Grandpa said the Bible is full of fairy tales."

"He really said that?" Cindi Arabie could feel a wave of anger rising within her. Realizing her kids were looking intently at her, she took a deep breath and tried to be calm.

"Look, I know Grandpa acts like he's not interested in spiritual matters, but we have to keep praying. God can change his heart. Look what happened to Mr. Canales."

Karin looked puzzled. "The guy who hands out the bulletins at church? What about him?"

Brad almost choked on his mashed potatoes. "Oh yeah! He was a real live criminal. He even robbed a drugstore!"

Karin's eyes got big. "You're kidding!"

"No, Brad's right. But the point is that while he was in prison, Mr. Canales gave his heart to the Lord."

"So what does this have to do with Grandpa?" Brad wondered.

"This," Cindi replied. "If God can touch the life of someone like Mr. Canales, he can certainly change Grandpa's heart."

⟳ Talk about It

- Who do you know who seems far away from God?
- What in your life seems like an "impossible situation"?
- How can those who love Jesus reach out to those who don't seem to care about Jesus?

☑ Check It Out

For a good reminder of the fact that God can do anything, read Genesis 18:10-14.

♡ Apply It

"Is anything too hard for the Lord?" The obvious answer is, "Of course not!" This question reveals much about God. Make it a habit to insert your specific needs into the question. "Is this day in my life too hard for the Lord?" "Is this habit I'm trying to break too hard for him?" "Is the communication problem I'm having too hard for him?" "Does it seem impossible that this person I'm praying for will ever believe?" Asking the question this way reminds us that God is personally involved in our lives and nudges us to ask for his power to help in the "impossible." A situation that seems impossible with human resources is simply an opportunity for God. When something seems impossible, keep praying, do what you can, and ask God to do the rest. He may see fit to make the impossible happen.

👥 Tip for Parents

Consider making a prayer list of friends and family members who need Christ.

God's Presence

It's August 29, and the mood at the Wellses' home is tense. You can sense the apprehension in the air. Everyone's on edge.

Mrs. Wells is trying her best to be upbeat and positive. She serves a big breakfast—sausage and eggs and biscuits—to her two sons.

Mark barely touches his food. Every now and then, he takes a sip of juice. But mostly he just stares out the window.

Brian, on the other hand, is filled with nervous energy. His right leg is bouncing up and down at woodpecker speed. He's peppering his mom with nonstop questions.

"What time does school start? How long does it take to get there? What's my teacher's name? Did you put some cookies in my lunch? Where are we supposed to meet you after school?"

Mrs. Wells patiently answers her son's queries. *This is so hard for them,* she thinks. *Being in a new place, going to a brand-new school, having to make all new friends. I wish there was something I could say. I know they're both scared to death.*

○ Talk about It

- How does it feel to move to a new place or go to a new school? Talk about your experiences.
- When you are nervous, do you get quiet like Mark or do you bounce around like Brian? Why?
- Why is it so hard for most people to adjust to change—to new situations?
- What could Mrs. Wells say to comfort her sons?
- Who do you know who is new in town or at church or school? What could you do to make that person feel at ease?

☑ Check It Out

Whenever we face scary times or new situations, it helps to remember that God is with us. See Isaiah 42:2-3 and Hebrews 13:5.

♡ Apply It

Fear is a dark shadow that envelops us and, in the end, traps us. Each of us has been a prisoner of fear at one time or another—fear of rejection, fear of being misunderstood, fear of uncertainty, fear of sickness, or even fear of death. But we can conquer fear by remembering the presence of the Lord with us. If we want to dispel the darkness of fear, let us remember with the psalmist that "the Lord is my light and my salvation" (Psalm 27:1).

♙♙ Tip for Parents

When we name our fears, we diminish their power over us. Teach your children to talk openly about their concerns. Admit the things that scare you. Let them see you wrestling with and praying about the uncertainties of life. When a child senses that "Mom and Dad know just how I feel," he or she experiences tremendous relief.

God's Will

It's early August, and Martha Roberson is in a tizzy. Her dilemma? Where to send her six-year-old son, Teddy, to school for first grade.

She could send him to the elementary school down the street. It's got a pretty good reputation—several Christian teachers and administrators. But it is also huge. And Martha's not very comfortable with some of the things she's heard on Christian radio about the direction in which public schools are going.

There's a private school in town. It's got a good academic reputation, and several friends send their children there. But on the downside, it is *very* expensive. Martha, assuming she could pay the steep tuition, worries about the long-term effect of sending a middle-class kid to an upper-class school.

Finally, there is a small Christian school. The people there are solid believers and well meaning, but Martha was not too impressed when she visited. It seemed more like Sunday school than "school school."

"Lord, what should I do?" Martha prays. "I want Teddy to be challenged academically but in an environment that is *friendly* to our spiritual beliefs. Right now it looks like I can have either one or the other! Please show me what's best."

○ Talk about It

- What do Christians mean when they talk about "God's will"?
- Talk about a time in your life when you know you were right in the middle of God's will.
- Have you ever realized that you were not in God's will? What did you do?
- What are some areas in your life where you struggle trying to find out God's will?
- What do you think God's will is regarding Teddy's schooling? Why?

☑ Check It Out

God doesn't want his will for our lives to be a deep, dark secret—he wants us to know it! See Romans 12:2; Colossians 1:9; and Psalm 143:10.

♡ Apply It

When the Israelites were traveling in the wilderness, they moved and camped as God guided (Numbers 9:23). When you follow God's guidance, you know you are where God wants you whether you're moving or staying in one place. You are physically somewhere right now. Instead of praying, "God, what do you want me to do next?" ask, "God, what do you want me to do while I'm right here?" Direction from God is not just for your next big move. He has a purpose for you now, where you are. Begin to fulfill God's purpose for your life by doing what he wants you to do now!

♦♦ Tip for Parents

Whether for yourself or for your children, discerning God's will usually involves one or more of these *C*-words: *counsel* (from God—via much prayer, as well as from older, wiser Christians), *circumstances* (trusting that God has you where you are for a reason), *common sense, compulsion* (inner promptings by the Spirit of God), and *contentment* (an unmistakable peace).

Good Works

Everybody in the Hunt family has a different opinion about the upcoming rummage sale/fund-raiser for the new Crisis Pregnancy Center in town.

Mr. Hunt is thinking about the fact that, for the first time in fourteen years, he'll be missing the opening day of deer season. "Out of fifty-two Saturdays in the year, they picked this one. I can't believe it!"

Brittany is feeling that the effort might be futile. "I heard we'll need to raise six hundred dollars just to pay the CPC's rent for one month! Last time we did something like this, we only earned about four hundred and fifty dollars. That's all! And we worked our tails off, too—for two whole days! I know it's important to help other people, but sometimes I feel like, 'what good's it going to do?'"

Daniel is claiming he's too busy to help. "I've got soccer practice. And also, I need to go to the library to work on my term paper. And on top of all that, I may have to go in and work for a couple of hours. Several people on the schedule have the flu."

⟳ Talk about It

- When is the last time you did something to help someone else? How did you feel afterward?
- Why is it important for Christians to serve other people and help those in need?
- What do you think about the attitudes of the members of the Hunt family? Can you relate to any of them? Why?
- What are some valid excuses for *not* serving others? What are some invalid excuses?
- What should be our motivation and attitude when we do "good works"?
- What is something you could do this week to help someone?

☑ Check It Out

Read the challenging commands in Galatians 6:8 and 1 Peter 2:12.

♡ Apply It

No Christian should ever think that he or she is totally independent and doesn't need help from others, and no one should feel excused from the task of helping others (Galatians 6:1-3). The body of Christ—the church—functions only when the members work together for the common good. Do you know someone who needs help? Is there a Christian brother or sister who needs correction or encouragement? Humbly and gently reach out to that person (John 13:34-35).

👥 Tip for Parents

Combat the common kid complaint that "there's nothing to do!" There is *always* something to do—especially when you consider the needs of others. Make it a rule at your house (on rainy days especially) that you will actively seek out someone in need and serve that person. Missionary care packages, notes of encouragement, errands for the elderly, a meal for someone who's sick—if our children grow up seeing these kinds of "good works" being modeled, they will embrace a servant-hearted, other-centered lifestyle.

Government

Is it just Greg's imagination, or are people becoming more and more antigovernment? Consider:

- On the news lately, there have been lots of stories about "militia movements." These are groups of people who think the government has too much power and who, in some cases, have even stopped paying taxes to the IRS.
- A number of prominent citizens and businessmen are forming a new political party to "fundamentally change the way government works and the way it is structured."
- Outside a football stadium recently, a group of people were giving out pamphlets that urged Christians to pray for God's punishment to fall on corrupt politicians and judges.

All this has Greg wondering: *How should a Christian view government?*

✪ Talk about It

- What are some good things government does for us?
- What are some ways government needs to change?
- If you could design a perfect government, what would it look like and do?
- When is it acceptable for Christians to disobey the law?
- What should Christians do if they disagree with certain laws or policies?
- How much involvement should Christians have in politics?

☑ Check It Out

Read some verses that describe how Christians should respond to civil authority—Romans 13:1-7; 1 Peter 2:17; and 1 Timothy 2:1-2.

♡ Apply It

When Peter told his readers to submit to the civil authorities (1 Peter 2:13-17), he was speaking of the Roman empire under Nero, a notoriously cruel tyrant. He was not telling believers to compromise their obedience to God; as Peter had told the high priest years before, "We must obey God rather than human authority" (Acts 5:29). But in most aspects of daily life, it was possible and desirable for Christians to live according to the law of their land. Today, some Christians live in freedom, while others live under repressive governments. All are commanded to cooperate with the rulers as far as conscience will allow. We are to do this for the Lord's sake—so that his Good News and his people will be respected. If we are to be persecuted, it should be for obeying God and not for breaking moral or civil laws.

♟ Tip for Parents

It is said that Rose Kennedy used to require her children to read the front page of the newspaper every morning before they came downstairs for breakfast. Each child had to be prepared to discuss and debate at least one current event. Is it any wonder that her children grew up to be so influential? You may not want to go to this extreme, but it is wise to teach your children to be aware of events and to be able to think about and evaluate culture from a Christian perspective.

Grades

When report cards came out last term, Christy Tolbert's grades were terrible. She just didn't try at all. So her parents laid down the law: no TV, no phone privileges, and no outside activities Monday through Thursday until the next report period.

Thus far the new studying strategy has worked. Christy has pulled up all her grades. In fact, if she does well on her big geography project (a report on the Everglades), she may even make the principal's honor roll.

Up late the night before the geography project is due, Christy is trying to copy her paper from the hard disk of her dad's computer onto a floppy disk—to save it. Somehow, she erases the whole paper, or the computer eats it, or the hard disk malfunctions. At any rate, the paper is gone!

Christy and her mom try unsuccessfully to recover the missing document. They call Mr. Tolbert (he is in Atlanta on a business trip). He suggests some other ways to try to save her paper. None of them work.

Now Christy is in tears. Even if she can piece together her disjointed scribbles and rewrite the whole thing, it'll be at least a day late. That'll mean a whole letter grade penalty.

"Daddy, I worked so hard!" she sobs. "And now my average will be all messed up! I probably won't make the honor roll."

Mr. Tolbert tries to comfort his discouraged daughter. "Sweetheart, I don't care so much about your grade. I care that you tried your best and that you learned something."

↻ Talk about It

- Which is more important—making good grades or learning about a subject? Why?
- How accurate are grades as an indicator of knowledge gained?
- What do you think God thinks of our society's emphasis on grades?
- What advice would you give to someone who was struggling in school?

☑ Check It Out

Discuss how the warning about laziness in Proverbs 12:24 applies to study habits.

♡ Apply It

In this age of information, knowledge is plentiful, but wisdom is scarce. Wisdom means far more than simply knowing a lot. It is a basic attitude that affects every aspect of life. The foundation of knowledge is to fear the Lord—to honor and respect God, to live in awe of his power, and to obey his Word. Faith in God should be the controlling principle for your understanding of the world, your attitudes, and your actions. Trust in God—he will make you truly wise.

♟ Tip for Parents

You can better motivate your children to study if you yourself will spend time "studying" each night. While they "hit the books," do some reading, learn a new skill, take a correspondence course, or get a review in the "three *R*s" (by helping your children with their homework).

Grandparents

Some words to describe recent events at the Jameses' house: *crazy, chaotic, unexpected, stressful,* and *difficult.*

What's going on? Mike's mom has moved in with the family. Her health has been failing for some time now, so the family has renovated the garage and made it into a small apartment. While the construction was taking place, Benjamin, twelve, and Anna, nine, had to share a bedroom in order to free up a room for their grandmother. That caused a *lot* of fireworks. Then a long-awaited family vacation had to be canceled. Six months into this new arrangement, everyone is still having a hard time adjusting to having Grandma James there all the time.

Tonight when Gina cooked turnip greens for Grandma and gave her a TV tray so she could watch a game show during dinner, Benjamin rolled his eyes and said in a low voice, "Wouldn't it be better for everybody if she just moved into a nursing home?"

Just then, Grandma called out from the living room, "Can someone come bring me some salt and pepper?"

○ Talk about It

- What are your favorite memories of your grandparents?
- Try to imagine being old and feeble. What would be hard about being elderly?
- Should children invite their parents to live with them in their later years, or should they recommend a nursing home? Why?
- Why is Grandma's presence causing so much friction in the Jameses' house?
- What advice would you give Mike, Gina, Benjamin, and Anna?

☑ Check It Out

Consider how eager Joseph was to be near and to care for his elderly father. Read Genesis 45:9-13.

♡ Apply It

The Pharisees of Jesus' day sponsored a practice known as *Corban* (literally, "offering"; see Matthew 15:5-6; Mark 7:11). Anyone who made a Corban vow was required to dedicate money to God's temple that otherwise would have gone to support his or her parents. Corban had become a religiously acceptable way to neglect parents, circumventing the child's responsibility to them. Although the action—giving money to God— seemed worthy and no doubt brought honor to the giver, many people who took the Corban vow were disobeying God's clear command to honor their parents. Don't let petty irritations, inconvenience, or cultural norms undermine your duty to honor your mother and father.

♙♙ Tip for Parents

Because people are living longer, it is highly likely that most Christians will face the dilemma of what to do with elderly parents. Be very careful and prayerful as you make these difficult decisions. Remember that your children are watching you and may one day duplicate your actions—with regard to you!

Gratefulness

For Kristen's seventh birthday, the Autreys went all out. A *surprise* slumber party with six of her best friends. Pizza. Cake and ice cream. Movies. And lots of gifts. Her big present? A new bike! The next morning, Kristen's dad even got up early and made bacon and pancakes for all the girls.

About an hour after everyone had left, the Autreys began to pick up the mess. Asked to take her new bike out onto the back porch, Kristen complained, "Why do *I* always have to do everything around here?"

"Excuse me," Kristen's mom said, "but I think we've spent the last twenty-four hours doing nothing but celebrate *your* birthday. Your dad and I knocked ourselves out to give you a fun day. I don't think it's asking very much to have you put your new bike where it belongs!"

"All right!" Kristen mumbled angrily. "I'll put the dumb ol' bike outside. It's not even the one I wanted anyway!"

◯ Talk about It

- Why do you think Kristen is in such a foul mood following such a fun birthday?
- What does it mean to be grateful? What are some specific ways to show gratitude?
- How would it make you feel to do something special for someone and then have them act like Kristen is acting?
- What should Kristen's parents do and say in this situation?
- Take a few minutes to list some things that you are grateful for today.

✉ Check It Out

The apostle Paul spent almost a whole chapter expressing his gratitude and appreciation to friends and coworkers. See Romans 16:1-16.

♡ Apply It

Ungratefulness creeps in whenever our sensors lock onto what we don't have. During their trip to the Promised Land, the people of Israel noticed not what God was doing for them—setting them free, making them a nation, giving them a new land—but what God was *not* doing for them (Numbers 11:4-6). They could think of nothing but the delicious Egyptian food they had left behind. Somehow they forgot that they had paid for that food with the brutal whip of Egyptian slavery, which had caused them to cry out to God for relief (Exodus 2:23). Are you grateful for what God has given you, or are you always thinking about what you would like to have? Don't allow your unfulfilled desires to kill your enjoyment of the life, food, health, work, and friends you do have. These are God's gifts, and they are good.

Tip for Parents

Instead of a perfunctory, rote prayer before meals, try having each family member complete this sentence: "Right now, I am grateful for _____." Then have someone lift all these expressions of appreciation to God in prayer.

Greed

As soon as Anne Griep dropped off her soon-to-be-eight-years-old son, Ryan, at a friend's birthday party, she knew she was in trouble.

It was an unbelievable affair—exotic decorations, a Spacewalk, a magician, pizza, and, of course, a veritable *mountain* of presents. "I should have expected this," Anne said to herself as she drove away from the lavish home situated in an exclusive neighborhood. "Brandon is the Claibornes' only child, and they had to wait a long time for him. . . . Hmmm, I can't wait to see how this affects Ryan. Especially since his birthday is in five weeks!"

Two hours later, Anne and Ryan were driving back home. Ryan had a bag of mere *party favors* easily worth fifteen to twenty dollars! And he talked nonstop about how much fun he had had and about all the cool presents Ryan got.

"Mom," he gushed, "what are we going to do for *my* birthday? I was thinking maybe we could have a cowboy party and even get some real horses and everything. And I think I'm big enough now for a BB gun. And, just think, if I invite as many people as Brandon, I'll get so many presents they won't even fit in my closet!"

Anne was disappointed and frustrated. "We'll have to talk about it later with your dad."

"No, Mom, let's talk about it right now!"

⟳ Talk about It

- What's the best birthday party you've ever been to? Why?
- Talk about a time when you felt jealous of someone else's things.
- What is greed? Why is greed not a good thing?
- What would you tell Ryan's mom if she came to you and said, "My son wants to have a big, expensive birthday party, and we can't afford to give him one. What should I do?"
- Do you think Ryan is being greedy? Why or why not?

☑ Check It Out

Read what Jesus said about possessions in Matthew 6:19-34.

♡ Apply It

Beware of greed. Lot's greedy desire for the best of everything led him into sinful surroundings (Genesis 13:10-11), and his experience is typical of how greed can ruin us. His burning desire for possessions and success cost him his freedom and enjoyment (Genesis 14:11-12). As King Kedorlaomer's captive, he could have been tortured, enslaved, or even killed. In much the same way, we can be enticed into doing things or going places we shouldn't. The prosperity we long for is captivating; it can both entice us and enslave us if our motives are not in line with God's desires.

♟ Tip for Parents

Fun does not have to be expensive. Besides, kids appreciate creativity as much as or more than extravagance. For a "space party," one dad built an "astronaut training" obstacle course in the family's backyard using ladders, ropes, chairs, a wheelbarrow, etc. It was the highlight of the party, and it didn't cost a thing!

Guilt

Eleven-year-old Ryan McCrery is having a hard time sleeping. He's been in bed for over an hour now, but he just keeps tossing and turning. This afternoon he went next door and cleaned out Mrs. Cheney's basement for her. She's getting older, and since her husband died last summer, she has to hire kids in the neighborhood to do odd jobs for her. Anyway, while Ryan was sweeping and straightening, he came across a box full of old baseball cards—a cardboard box stuffed to the top! At least five thousand cards. Maybe even more!

Ryan couldn't believe it. For thirty minutes his heart raced as he thumbed through the collection. It was like taking a trip through the Hall of Fame—Koufax, Williams, Mantle, Clemente, Aaron, Gibson. Not only were there some valuable cards, but there were even some duplicates!

Before Ryan even knew what he was doing, he found himself taking fifteen or twenty of the duplicate cards and putting them in his coat pocket. Then he finished cleaning up and hurried home.

So now you know why Ryan's having a hard time sleeping. And now you know why every few minutes he sits up in bed and glances over toward his jacket hanging there on the back of his desk chair.

⟳ Talk about It

- What does it mean to be guilty?
- Is guilt just a feeling? Why or why not?
- When was the last time you felt really guilty? What happened?
- If Ryan came to you and told you his story and asked your advice, what would you say to him?
- What is the best solution for someone who feels guilty?

☑ Check It Out

The Bible makes it clear—we don't have to live under a pile of guilt. There *is* a way out. See Psalm 130:3-4; Jeremiah 3:22; Micah 7:18-19; and, of course, 1 John 1:9.

♡ Apply It

After sinning, Adam and Eve felt guilt and embarrassment over their nakedness (Genesis 3:7-8). Their guilty feelings made them try to hide from God. A guilty conscience is a warning signal God placed inside you that goes off when you've done wrong. The worst step you could take is to eliminate the guilty feelings without eliminating the cause. That would be like using a painkiller but not treating the cause of the pain. Be glad those guilty feelings are there. They make you aware of your sin so you can ask God's forgiveness and then correct your wrongdoing.

♟ Tip for Parents

We're often inclined to think we must hide our mistakes from our children. After all, if they know about the wrong choices we've made, they might rationalize, "Hey, Mom (or Dad) did this once. That means I can do it, too!" That is a parenting myth. By sharing our regret over past (and present) failures, our children see us as real and approachable. Give your kids the benefit of both your good *and* your bad experiences.

Heaven

Watching cartoons one rainy Saturday morning, seven-year-old Evan begins wondering about heaven. Why? One of the characters got blown up, and the cartoon ended with him dressed in white, sitting on a cloud, playing the harp.

"Mom, is that heaven?"

"Is what heaven?"

"You know, like on the cartoon. That dog was up in the clouds, playing the harp like an angel."

"Well, that's a good question. Nobody really knows where heaven is."

"Is it up in the sky?"

"Well, I don't know. But I know Jesus went up into the sky when he left the earth. So maybe it is up. I just know heaven is wherever God is."

"Oh. . . . So what will we *do* in heaven? Will we be playing harps and stuff?"

"Hmmm. It's hard to say. I know we'll be worshiping God."

"Oh. So does that mean heaven is like church?"

"I guess in some ways."

"And so we're just gonna sit around forever and sing and pray?"

"Well, I don't know about that. I think the Bible mentions that we will rest in heaven."

"That's a long time to be resting. Wouldn't we get tired of that?"

"Yeah, well, that's not all we'll be doing."

"What else, then?"

"I'm not exactly sure. I think the Bible says something about us serving God."

"Mom, is heaven gonna be fun?"

"Evan, you're asking some great questions. And I'm sorry I don't know all the answers. But I do know the answer to that question—yes, heaven is going to be the best place ever. It will be more fun than you can imagine."

◯ Talk about It

- Do you think much about heaven?
- Sometimes people use the word *eternity*. What does that mean?
- What do you think heaven is going to be like?
- How can a person know for sure whether he or she is going to heaven?
- What can we do on earth to get ready for living in heaven?
- Are you going to heaven? How do you know?

✉ Check It Out

Explore these facts about heaven: God is there (Matthew 6:9); it is a place of pure joy (Revelation 21:3-4 and 22:3-5); we are to be heavenly minded while we live on this earth (Matthew 6:19-21; Colossians 3:2).

♡ Apply It

As believers, we are "foreigners and aliens" in this world because our real home is with God (1 Peter 2:11). Heaven is not the cloud-and-harp existence favored by cartoonists. Heaven is where God lives. Life in heaven operates according to God's principles and values, and it is eternal and unshakable. Heaven came to earth in the symbolism of the Jewish sanctuary (the tabernacle and temple) where God's presence dwelt. It came in a fuller way in the person of Jesus Christ, "God with us." It permeated the entire world as the Holy Spirit came to live in every believer.

❙❙ Tip for Parents

Discussions about heaven are prime opportunities to explain the gospel to your children. Don't just *talk* about eternal glory; show them how they can enter into it through trusting in Jesus. Before they can make these kinds of faith decisions they will need to understand and grapple with their sinfulness and what its consequences are, the death of Christ and why it was necessary, faith and what it means to believe. Share the truth little by little and pray. Over time the Spirit of God can help your children put it all together and ultimately come to a saving knowledge of Christ.

Hell

The sermon at church on Sunday morning was all about hell.

Needless to say, conversation around the dinner table was very interesting that afternoon.

"Sandy says there's no such place."

"What? How can she make a dumb statement like that?"

"I don't know. But she just thinks that if God is all-loving, then he would never send anyone to a terrible place like that."

"You need to tell Sandy what Reverend Claunch said."

"Which part?"

"You know, the part about Jesus talking way more about hell than he ever did about heaven."

"Oh yeah, that was good."

"I mean, if there is no such place as hell, then why did Jesus talk so much about it?"

○ Talk about It

- What do you think of when you hear the word *hell?*
- Why are people reluctant to believe in the reality of hell?
- How can you work this week to point people to heaven instead of to hell?

☑ Check It Out

Assign family members to read the following passages about hell: Matthew 5:29-30; 2 Peter 2:4; 2 Thessalonians 1:7-9; and Revelation 14:9-11.

♡ Apply It

Jesus said quite plainly that "eternal punishment" awaits those who do not know God (Matthew 25:46). Eternal punishment takes place in hell (the lake of fire, or Gehenna), the place of punishment after death for all those who refuse to repent.

In the Bible, three words are used in connection with eternal punishment. (1) *Sheol,* or "the grave," is used in the Old Testament to mean the place of the dead, generally thought to be under the earth (see Job 24:19; Psalm 16:10; Isaiah 38:10). (2) *Hades* is the Greek word for "the underworld," the realm of the dead. It is the word used in the New Testament for Sheol (see Matthew 16:18; Revelation 1:18; 20:13-14). (3) *Gehenna,* or "hell," was named after the valley of Ben-hinnom near Jerusalem, where children were sacrificed by fire to the pagan gods (see 2 Kings 23:10; 2 Chronicles 28:3). This is the place of eternal fire (Matthew 5:22; 10:28; Mark 9:43; Luke 12:5; James 3:6; Revelation 19:20), prepared for the devil, his angels, and all those who do not believe in God (Matthew 25:46; Revelation 20:10). This is the final and eternal destination of all those who reject God.

When Jesus warns against unbelief, he is trying to save us from agonizing punishment.

♛ Tip for Parents

Discussions of hell can be terrifying to children. We need to walk that fine line between honestly presenting sobering truth and "scaring them into the kingdom." Hell is a real, horrible, and permanent place. Our children need to see it in all of its stark awfulness. But they also need to know of God's wonderful provision of salvation and a heavenly home that is too beautiful for description.

Holiness

During a weekend trip to Grandma's, the following exchange takes place between ten-year-old Ashley and her father.

"Daddy?"

"What, babe?"

"What's the speed limit on this road?"

"Uh, I think it's sixty-five."

"So how fast are you going?"

Mr. Morris can tell where this conversation is headed. "Uh, about seventy-one." (It's actually more like seventy-three.)

"So isn't that speeding?"

"Well, I guess technically it is, but there's kind of this unwritten rule that the police won't stop you as long as you're within 10 percent of the speed limit."

Mrs. Morris rolls her eyes. She's trying not to laugh. But Ashley is persistent.

"But, Daddy, what do the *written* rules say?"

"You mean the highway signs?"

"Yes, sir."

"They say '65.' You're supposed to go '65.'"

"So shouldn't you be doing that?"

Mr. Morris is uncomfortable and a bit annoyed. He feels like he's being grilled by a ten-year-old prosecuting attorney. "Well, yeah, I guess so, but look at everybody else who's passing us like we're sitting still."

"But, Daddy, you always tell *me* that it doesn't matter what anybody else is doing. It just matters what you do."

"Yeah, yeah, OK, you're right, Ashley," Mr. Morris mumbles reluctantly. "Hey, is anybody else hungry?" he asks, changing the subject.

"Good idea," Mrs. Morris cracks. "How 'bout a big slice of humble pie?"

"Very funny!" Mr. Morris mumbles.

○ Talk about It

- Is it important to follow some of the rules or all of the rules? Why?
- What rules do you regard as not very important? Why?
- Why was Mr. Morris getting uncomfortable and annoyed at the questions his daughter Ashley was asking? Why did he try to change the subject?
- God tells us to turn away from all sins, not just certain sins. Why do we act like certain sins are "no big deal"?
- What rules do you need to pay more attention to today?

☑ Check It Out

Read and discuss 1 Peter 1:15-16 and then apply it to the situation above.

♡ Apply It

Committing our life to Christ does not eliminate the pull to live by our old ways. Yet Peter tells us to be like our heavenly Father—holy in everything we do (1 Peter 1:15-16). *Holiness* means being totally devoted or dedicated to God, set aside for his special use and set apart from sin and its influence. We're to be set apart and different, not blending in with the crowd, yet not being different just for the sake of being different. God's qualities in our lives are what make us different. Our focus and priorities must be his. All this is in direct contrast to our old ways (1:14). We cannot become holy on our own, but God gives us his Holy Spirit to help us obey and to give us power to overcome sin. Don't use the excuse that you can't help slipping into sin. Call on God's power to free you from sin's grip.

♛ Tip for Parents

When your children catch you in an inconsistency, resist the urge to make excuses or to justify your behavior. Rather, swallow your pride, freely admit that you're wrong, and turn the situation into a positive teaching moment. Let them see what humility and repentance look like in the life of a struggling but growing Christian.

Honesty

It is the third night of the Foreman visit, and the Humphreys have had just about all they can stand. The normally neat house is a wreck. The usually full refrigerator is empty. The typically organized laundry room is strewn with the clothes of the visiting family—all six of them! The Humphrey girls are complaining about spending another two nights on the lumpy sofa sleeper in the basement. The family cat is nowhere to be seen.

To complicate matters, the Humphreys' newborn is sick. In the darkness of the nursery, Wade rocks the newborn while his wife, Amy, changes the sheets in the crib.

"I can't take two more nights of this," Wade states flatly.

"You? I feel like a chef. I spent the day in the kitchen."

"Can't you say something to them? I mean, Sally is one of your best friends."

"Oh, right, Wade! What am I going to say? 'Uh, can you guys leave now because you're really driving us nuts?'"

Wade chuckles. "I guess you're right. It's a touchy situation."

Amy just sighs. Then she takes the baby from her husband and begins to nurse him.

Walking back into the living room where his guests are sprawled about watching TV, Wade immediately realizes something terrible. The nursery monitor is on! In all likelihood, his guests have just heard every word he and Amy have spoken!

○ Talk about It

- Do you agree with the old saying Honesty is the best policy? Why or why not?
- Why is it sometimes hard to be honest with others?
- Which is worse—to not say what you're thinking or to bluntly tell everything you are thinking? Why?
- What can be done to avoid weird situations like the one described above?

☑ Check It Out

Read Ephesians 4:15 and discuss the two qualities that ought to mark all our communication.

♡ Apply It

Christ is the truth (John 14:6), and the Holy Spirit who guides the church is the Spirit of truth (John 16:13). Satan, by contrast, is the father of lies (John 8:44). As followers of Christ, we must be committed to the truth. This means both that our words should be honest and that our actions should reflect Christ's integrity. Speaking the truth in love is not always easy, convenient, or pleasant, but it is necessary and is often the best course of action for everyone involved.

♟ Tip for Parents

It isn't just what we say but how we say it that counts. Researchers have shown that nonverbal communication (tone of voice, body language, facial expression, etc.) can easily overshadow the verbal!

Human Nature

The Mayhall family watched a TV program last night about crime and punishment. Reporters went inside prisons. They interviewed victims of crime. They talked with politicians. And then they talked to some social scientists about what makes people break the law and commit violent acts.

Jason was shocked to hear one scholarly looking sociologist assert, "There is *absolutely no* evidence that people have a propensity to commit crime. It is *society* that creates criminals. And I can demonstrate it for you. Take identical-twin orphans and put one in an upper-class home where he or she is loved and nurtured, and place the other one in a welfare home in the inner city. I don't have to tell you what is likely to happen. The child who grows up in the good environment will most likely turn out OK. And the child who grows up in poverty amidst the violent world of the city will very likely be influenced into antisocial behavior. It might make for a good *sermon* to preach that people are intrinsically evil, but that idea has no basis in fact. It's a religious myth. I prefer to believe in the innate goodness of man and the essential corruptness of the social order."

Jason's wife, Deanne, shook her head in disgust, grabbed the remote control, and clicked off the TV. "Ohhh, that makes me so mad!"

"What does, Mom?" eleven-year-old Mary inquired.

○ Talk about It

- Talk about the crime problem in your city. What would you do (if you were the mayor) to improve it?
- In the program that the Mayhalls watched, what was the sociologist trying to say?
- Do you think people are basically good or basically sinful? Why? What evidence can you give to support your view?
- Never before has a society had so many laws, law-enforcement officers, and prisons. And yet crime rates continue to climb. Why? What is the problem?
- What sins do you need to confess to God today?

☑ Check It Out

In discussing the nature of mankind, consider these verses: Ephesians 2:3; Romans 3:23; Isaiah 53:6 and 64:6.

♡ Apply It

Before we believed in Christ, our nature was evil. We disobeyed, rebelled, and ignored God. (Even at our best, we did not love him with all our heart, soul, and mind.) The Christian, however, has a new nature. God has crucified the old, rebellious nature (Romans 6:6) and replaced it with a new loving nature. The penalty of sin died with Christ on the cross. God has declared us not guilty, and we need no longer live under sin's power (Colossians 2:12-15). God does not take us out of the world or make us robots—we will still feel like sinning, and sometimes we will sin. The difference lies in our options—before we were saved, we were slaves to our sinful nature; now we are free to live for Christ (Galatians 2:20).

Tip for Parents

Moody Bible Institute has produced a number of award-winning videos that look at scientific issues from a Christian perspective. You might want to call or write for a free catalog. Write to:

Moody Video
820 N. LaSalle Street
Chicago, IL 60610
(800) 842-1223.

Hunger

Channel surfing together one night, Stan Smith and his seven-year-old son, Brock, come across a TV program about world hunger. After seeing about five seconds' worth of bony children with bloated bellies, Stan flicks the remote.

"Dad! Go back!"

"Why?"

"I want to see that show."

"What show?" Stan asks, trying to play dumb.

"The one with the little kids."

"Aw, Brock. You don't need to see that."

"Why not?"

"Well, it's just not for kids."

"But it was all *about* kids."

"Well, yeah, but—"

"Dad, why were they so skinny?"

"Well, because, um . . . I guess, because they, uh, don't have any food."

Brock is shocked. "What do you mean, they don't have any food?"

"Well, I mean they live in poor countries, and sometimes they don't have moms and dads. Or maybe there's a war going on. Or a drought."

"You mean they don't eat *ever?* What happens to them?"

"Uh, Brock, well, it's kind of hard to talk about. I mean, sometimes they—"

"Dad, if *I* didn't have food to eat, I would die, wouldn't I?"

"Well, after a while, yeah, you would."

"Dad, we've got to do something! We've got to help them!"

↻ Talk about It

- What is the longest period of time you have ever gone without food? What was it like?
- Why do you think Brock's dad felt uncomfortable talking about hungry children?
- Brock wants to help. How could he do that?
- Has your family ever helped feed the hungry? How? What happened?

☑ Check It Out

Prayerfully consider how you might help feed someone who is hungry in light of verses like Proverbs 29:7 and Isaiah 58:10-12.

♡ Apply It

King David once wrote, "I have never seen the godly forsaken, nor seen their children begging for bread" (Psalm 37:25). In David's day, Israel obeyed God's laws that ensured that the poor were treated fairly and mercifully. As long as Israel was obedient, there was enough food for everyone. Whenever Israel forgot God, the rich took care only of themselves, and the poor suffered (Amos 2:6-7).

Whenever we see a Christian brother or sister suffering, we can respond in one of three ways. (1) We can say, as Job's friends did, that the afflicted person brought this on himself. (2) We can say that this is a test to help the poor develop more patience and trust in God. (3) We can help the person in need. God would approve of only the last option. Although many governments today have programs for helping people in need, this is no excuse for ignoring the poor and needy within our reach.

♟ Tip for Parents

As a family project you may want to consider sponsoring a Compassion child. For less than a dollar a day you can "adopt" a child and provide him or her with food, basic medical care, and Christian schooling. You can even correspond with your child on a regular basis. For more information, write to:

Compassion International
3955 Cragwood Drive
P.O. Box 7000
Colorado Springs, CO 80933

Idolatry

The Harrisons attend church together regularly. They pray before meals and have a family devotional time every week. The parents teach Sunday school, and the kids wear Christian T-shirts to school.

It appears the Harrisons are very committed to Christ. But take a closer look at their individual pursuits and interests.

Mike Harrison spends almost every free moment he has restoring a 1966 Mustang. He stays up late and gets up early to refurbish and polish and tinker with his beloved car.

Kathy is consumed with things like curtains and dust ruffles. She spends hours each week browsing in furniture stores, looking at wallpaper samples, or doing home improvement projects. Friends remark that "something is different about your home every time we come over!"

Fifteen-year-old P. J. has one thing on her mind—her boyfriend, Clay. They talk on the phone for hours each night, and they are together every chance they get. P. J.'s room is like a "Clay" shrine—the walls are covered with pictures of him.

And what is eleven-year-old Bret's obsession? Sports. If he's not outside playing whatever game is in season, he is inside watching the sports channel on cable. At night he lies in bed and dreams of a career in the NBA. His goal in life? Easy. To dunk a ten-foot goal.

⟳ Talk about It

- What hobbies or interests do you have (or would you like to have)?
- How can a person tell if hobbies or interests have become too important or too consuming?
- How can you tell what is the most important thing in a person's life?
- Does living for Christ mean that you can't enjoy other things?

☑ Check It Out

Read Exodus 20:1-5 and talk about what it means to let something become an "idol" in our life today.

♡ Apply It

When God gave Israel the Ten Commandments, the Israelites had just come from Egypt, a land of many idols and many gods. Because each god represented a different aspect of life, it was common to worship many gods in order to get the maximum number of blessings. When God told his people to worship and believe in him, that wasn't so hard for them—he was just one more god to add to the list. But when he said, "You shall have no other gods before me," that was difficult for the people to accept. But if they didn't learn that the God who led them out of Egypt was the only true God, they could not be his people—no matter how faithfully they kept the other nine commandments. Thus, God made this his first commandment and emphasized it more than the others. Today we can allow many things to become gods to us. Money, fame, work, or pleasure can become gods when we concentrate too much on them for personal identity, meaning, and security. No one sets out with the intention of worshiping these things. But as we devote more and more time to them, they can grow into gods that ultimately control our thoughts and energies. Letting God hold the central place in our lives keeps these things from turning into gods.

👥 Tip for Parents

Regardless of what we say is most important, our life will show what we value by how we spend our time and how we spend our money. Before you accuse your children of "wasting time doing stupid things," examine your own life.

Impact

People all over town know who Beverly Simpson is.

She's the housewife and mother of two who petitioned the local cable-TV company to drop several channels that show nasty movies. She never meant to start a crusade, and she sure wasn't trying to become an object of household conversation in Summerfield.

Nevertheless, here she is. Some people applaud her courage and have joined in her fight for decency. Others have labeled her a right-wing fanatic and a prude.

What does Mrs. Simpson think? If she had known her actions were going to cause such a stir, would she still have tackled this issue?

"It's been hard on the whole family. The kids have been teased at school. We've received a couple of obscene phone calls. But, even with all that, I'd do it over again. I don't think I've been ugly or pushy. I just shared my concerns and got some other people to join with me.

"And I don't know what will eventually happen. But at least I can sleep easy knowing I did what I could. I tried to make a difference."

☼ Talk about It

- What do you think about people like Mrs. Simpson?
- How much should Christians be involved in trying to "clean up" society? Is it realistic to expect non-Christians to adhere to our moral values and beliefs?
- Do you think petitions and/or boycotts work? Why or why not?
- How would you feel if your mom (or dad) became involved in something like the situation described above?
- What are some issues about which you feel so strongly that you must speak up? Why do you single out these issues?
- Can kids or teenagers make a difference in their schools or in society at large? If so, how?

☑ Check It Out

Read about Christ's command for Christians to make a difference in the world by being "salt and light"—Matthew 5:13-16.

♡ Apply It

If a seasoning has no flavor, it has no value. If Christians make no effort to affect the world around them, they are of little value to God. If they are too much like the world, they are worthless. Christians should not blend in with everyone else. They should affect others positively, just as seasoning brings out the best flavor in food.

Can you hide a city that is sitting on top of a hill? Its light at night can be seen for miles. If we live for Christ, we will glow like lights, showing others what Christ is like. We hide our light whenever we (1) stay quiet about our Christian point of view when we should speak about it, (2) go along with the crowd when we should go against it, (3) compromise our Christian duty for the sake of a cultural rule or "obligation," (4) sin, or (5) ignore the needs of others. Be a beacon of truth—don't shut your light off from the rest of the world.

♟♟ Tip for Parents

The world is getting more and more perverted and sick all the time. No one can do everything, but each of us can do something. We can pray. We can share our faith. We can speak out. We can rear godly kids. Ask God what specific issues and what specific actions you need to engage in.

Initiative

If there's one thing characteristic of the Packman family, it's that they're all a bunch of go-getters.

When Bob sees something broken around the house, he tends to fix it before his wife, Kathy, can even put it on her "honey-do" list (sometimes before she even knows anything is wrong!).

When son Michael receives a long-term assignment at school, he immediately jumps all over it, breaking it down into manageable pieces. Invariably he completes book reports and term papers days ahead of schedule. Just when all his classmates are starting to sweat, he's kicking back and relaxing.

Daughter Gwen is an invaluable member of the youth group. She's always coming up with ideas for making the youth room or the meetings better. Like Radar O'Reilly, the company clerk on the old TV show *M*A*S*H*, she does needed tasks before the youth leaders can even ask.

○ Talk about It

- What is initiative, and why is it important?
- In what ways could too much initiative be a negative thing?
- What members of your family tend to take initiative most? Why?
- What is the opposite of taking initiative?
- How can initiative help make a family better?
- What are some practical ways you can take initiative this week?

☑ Check It Out

Read Proverbs 6:6-8, a great passage about taking initiative.

♡ Apply It

Ruth in the Bible took initiative and worked hard (Ruth 2:8-9). She knew, as all go-getters do, that sometimes hard work with little rest is our only option. Boaz noticed Ruth's hard work. Had she considered herself too proud or embarrassed to glean, she would have missed the opportunity to meet Boaz, change her life, and become the ancestor to a king and the Messiah. Taking initiative is a good thing!

▮▮ Tip for Parents

More and more employers seem to be looking for workers who are self-starters. This means we do our children a great service if we teach them to observe carefully, solve problems wisely, and work diligently. The kid who does things well—without being told—will almost always go farther than those who require constant supervision. Much of this hinges on personality, but initiative can be, to some extent, an acquired trait.

Integrity

Jim Peters and his son, Robbie, have finally found the computer they want. It has everything they've been looking for—speed, a big color monitor, lots of memory, and a built-in CD-ROM drive.

They were preparing to order the system from a mail-order company when Jim bumped into his friend Dennis, who works for the local university.

Dennis: So, did you guys ever decide on a computer?

Jim: Yeah, we're planning to order the PC Pegasus 850 tomorrow.

Dennis: Really? That's a great system. Where are you getting it?

Jim: Some mail-order house—only $1,950! Can you believe?

Dennis: $1,950? Jim, I can beat that price.

Jim: How?

Dennis: Because I work at the university, I can get a special educational discount. I should be able to get the same setup for about $1800.

Jim: That's amazing!

Dennis: Yeah, you could just write me a check. I'd deposit it, and then I would turn around and write the school a check. They'd never know.

Jim (concerned): What do you mean, "They'd never know"?

Dennis: Well, you know, technically that special price is only for students, staff, and faculty, but people do this kind of thing all the time.

○ Talk about It

- What about Dennis's offer? Should Jim take it or not? Why?
- What factors make Dennis's offer hard to resist?
- What do you think Jim should say to Dennis?
- What is a situation in your life where you're tempted to bend the rules a little bit?
- As a family, how can we encourage each other to have integrity?

☑ Check It Out

Read about the integrity of the prophet Daniel in Daniel 6:1-5.

♡ Apply It

A blameless life is far more valuable than wealth, but most people don't act as if they believe this. Afraid of not getting everything they want, they will pay any price to increase their wealth—cheating on their taxes, stealing from stores or employers, withholding tithes, refusing to give. But when we know and love God, we realize that a lower standard of living— or even poverty—is a small price to pay for personal integrity. Do your actions show that you sacrifice your integrity to increase your wealth? What changes do you need to make in order to get your priorities straight?

Tip for Parents

We live in an age that couldn't care less about what is right. Instead, the prevailing philosophy seems to be *what can I get away with?* Make the effort to teach your children the difference between right and wrong. Then model that kind of behavior for them.

Involvement

Pamela was in the grocery store with her fourteen-year-old daughter, Sarah, when she spied a shocking magazine cover. What made it especially offensive was the fact that the popular model in the picture was wearing a nun's habit, and yet she was in the arms of a famous actor.

Pamela was incensed! The pose of the models by itself was practically pornographic, but the fact that the magazine had the woman dressed as a nun made it blasphemous.

"I'm not going to stand for this!" Pamela announced.

"Mom," Sarah said with a gulp, "what are you going to do?"

"I'm going to tell the manager of the store that I resent him stocking and selling a magazine like this."

"Mom! You're not going to make a big scene, are you?"

"I'm going to do what I have to do."

"Well, can I go out to the car then?"

"No, I want you to come with me."

Pamela marches over to the manager's office and knocks on the door. Sarah stands about fifteen feet away, trying to be inconspicuous.

As her mom begins telling the manager that she is offended by the magazine, several shoppers begin watching the confrontation.

Just then one of the bag boys—a guy Sarah knows from school—comes over to observe the scene.

Sarah turns beet red!

○ Talk about It

- Why do you think Sarah was embarrassed in this situation?
- Could you (or would you) do what Pamela did? Why or why not?
- How should Christians react to filthy magazines or TV programs?
- Should we speak out? Why or why not?
- Why do you think our society is becoming more and more interested in magazines and pictures like the one described above?

☑ Check It Out

Have someone in your family read Ephesians 5:8-15.

♡ Apply It

It is important to avoid the "fruitless deeds of darkness" (any pleasure or activity that results in sin), but we must go even further than that. Paul instructs us to *expose* these deeds, because our silence may be interpreted as approval. God needs people who will take a stand for what is right. Evil is pervasive in our society, to the point where we look askance instead of being appalled and angered by it. We must keep our standards high and speak out when we need to.

▮▮ Tip for Parents

When objecting (either in person, by phone, or by letter) to practices of a store, TV station, advertiser, public official, etc., make sure that you do so in a controlled, Christlike manner. Let your children see that confrontations do not have to degenerate into explosive, name-calling episodes.

Irritations

It's a rainy Saturday (the third wet day in a row), and the whole Madsen family is cooped up inside—together.

Everyone is starting to get edgy. Nerves are jangled. Tempers are short. There's nowhere to go to get away.

Samantha feels claustrophobic—as if she's going to start screaming at any moment. Her mom insists on playing some fuddy-duddy CD—big-band music from the forties. And her brother, Kevin, keeps bugging her. One minute he's popping her with a towel; the next time she turns around he's shooting her with a water pistol. She's asked him to stop a couple of times, but he keeps at it.

Just now her dad has entered the room and wants the whole family to go down into the basement to do some serious cleaning.

Sam's mom protests immediately, and the two begin arguing. Just then Kevin sneaks up and whops Sam in the face with a pillow.

◯ Talk about It

- Why do family members tend to get on each other's nerves so easily?
- What are some of the irritating things that your parents/siblings do?
- What could your family do to lessen the friction in your home?
- Have you ever felt like Samantha? When? What happened?
- How do you feel when members of your family start arguing?
- Talk about a time when your family got along really well. What was the secret to that cooperation and peace?

☑ Check It Out

Ephesians 4:2 and 1 Thessalonians 5:13-15 give us some good reminders of how to minimize family friction.

♡ Apply It

It would be great if peace came to us whenever we wanted it, with no effort or cost involved. But as King David explained, we must seek and pursue peace (Psalm 34:14). Paul echoed this thought in Romans 12:18. Any person who wants peace must not argue or fight. Because peaceful relationships come from our efforts to make peace, try hard to live in peace with others each day. Refuse to fight with those who pick fights.

▮▮ Tip for Parents

In recent years, publishers have come out with a number of books for families with titles like *101 Things to Do on a Rainy Day* and *Projects for Family Fun.* Such a book can be a good investment. Every mom and dad needs a little creative help for those times when the children are fidgety and fussy. Go to a bookstore or a teachers' supply store for those kinds of resources.

Kindness

During lunch Russ called home and said, "Mom, I have to have my game uniform washed in time for practice this afternoon. Coach told us we're taking pictures."

"Russ, when did the coach tell you this?"

"I dunno. Last week I think."

"And you're just now telling me? That's less than three hours from now."

"Sorry, Mom, but I gotta have it."

Mrs. Bryce drops off the clean uniform and gets over to the junior high just in time to pick up her daughter, Michelle. Halfway home, Michelle gasps, "Oh, Mom! I almost forgot. I've got to go the library and photocopy an article for my government class."

"But, Michelle, I've got to get home. The wallpaper guy is supposed to call between 3:45 and 4:00."

"Mommm! If I don't get that article, I'll get a zero on my homework assignment. Do you want me to flunk?"

At supper Mr. Bryce doesn't say much except to note that "the roast is kinda tough tonight, honey. What happened?"

Everyone is shocked when Mrs. Bryce buries her face in her napkin and then leaves the dinner table sobbing.

⟳ Talk about It

- Why do you think Mrs. Bryce got so upset?
- What, if anything, was wrong with the way Russ, Michelle, and Mr. Bryce approached their mom/wife?
- What are some ways you have failed to show kindness lately to your fellow family members?
- What are some things you could do today or this week to be more kind at home?

☑ Check It Out

Relate Colossians 3:12-17 to the story above and to your own family situation.

♡ Apply It

If our faith in Christ is real, it will usually prove itself at home, in our relationships with those who know us best. Ideally, Christian parents and Christian children will relate to each other with thoughtfulness and love. This will happen if both parents and children put the others' interests above their own—that is, if they submit to one another. In Colossians 3:12-17, Paul offers a strategy to help us live for God day by day: (1) Imitate Christ's compassionate, forgiving attitude (3:12-13); (2) let love guide your life (3:14); (3) let the peace of Christ rule in your heart (3:15); (4) always be thankful (3:15); (5) keep God's Word in you at all times (3:16); and (6) live as Jesus Christ's representative (3:17). All the virtues that Paul encourages us to develop are perfectly bound together by love. As we clothe ourselves with these virtues, the last garment we are to put on is love, which holds all of the others in place. Examine your family relationships. Do you relate to one another as God intended?

♟♟ Tip for Parents

Kids generally don't mean to be unkind; they simply don't think. To avoid last-minute intrusions like the ones above, you may wish to institute a family scheduling session each week. This practice can help children learn how to plan ahead. It may also be necessary on occasion to let your children bear the consequences of their irresponsible behavior. Such lessons are hard but indelible!

Listening

As she walks out the door, Dell gives one final instruction to her husband, Tom. "When the buzzer goes off, put the casserole in the oven, OK?"

"Sure, honey!" Tom replies without looking up from the TV. He and his son Seth are engrossed in an exciting NFL play-off game.

Thirty minutes later, the buzzer sounds. Tom looks at his son and says, "What did she say that means?"

Seth shrugs. "I think she said we're supposed to let the dog out."

"Oh yeah."

An hour later, Dell walks in the door and sees the casserole sitting on the kitchen counter.

"Tom!"

○ Talk about It

- Why is listening such a hard thing to do?
- What are some things that make it hard to listen?
- Who is the best listener in your home? Who is the worst? Why?
- How do you feel when you really want and need to say something and nobody is really paying attention?
- What if God listened to our prayers only as well as we listen to each other?
- What are some practical ways we can improve our listening skills?

☑ Check It Out

Consider two verses that emphasize the importance of listening—James 1:19 and Proverbs 18:13.

♡ Apply It

The Bible tells us to be "quick to listen" (James 1:19). Whenever we fail to do that, we communicate to others that we think our priorities, needs, and wants are more important than theirs. James wisely advised us to reverse that. When people talk to you, make them feel that their viewpoints and ideas have value. Put aside the thoughts that keep you from paying attention to others when you should be listening to them. Ignore the distractions and make yourself listen.

▮▮ Tip for Parents

One way you can teach your children to listen is by using the acronym A-B-C. *A* stands for *ask questions. B* stands for *be attentive. C* stands for *confirm what others say* (i.e., repeat their feelings or statements back to them to make sure you are hearing them correctly). This simple method, if used with regularity, can go a long way toward training your children in the forgotten art of listening.

Loneliness

"I don't like this—not one bit! In fact, I hate it!" Terri complained.

"I know, sweetie. It's hard. But you did the right thing!" her mom insisted, trying to offer comfort.

"So if I did right, why does everyone treat me like I'm some kind of criminal? They, like, won't even *speak* to me. All the people who I thought were my friends have totally turned their backs on me."

"Terri, look. I'm proud of you. You went to the movies with a bunch of friends. You were supposed to be going to see a PG movie. And once you were all inside, your friends said, 'Let's go next door into the theater showing an R movie.' And you had the character and the courage to stand up to them and say, 'No. I'm not going to do that. It's wrong.' Terri, I think that's terrific. And I think you are terrific!"

"Well, gee, thanks, Mom. But I still feel pretty lonely."

⟳ Talk about It

- Talk about some times in your life when you felt lonely. What's the worst part about feeling all alone?
- Have you ever felt lonely for taking an unpopular stand? What happened?
- Would you have done what Terri did? (Be honest!) Why or why not?
- What are some situations coming up in your life in which if you do the right thing, you may end up feeling lonely?
- How can the rest of the family pray for you?

✉ Check It Out

Oftentimes, we will be lonely (and alone) when we choose to do the right thing. See Jeremiah 26:8 and 2 Timothy 3:12.

♡ Apply It

Judah's leaders persecuted Jeremiah repeatedly for faithfully proclaiming God's messages (Jeremiah 38:6). For forty years of faithful ministry, he received no acclaim, no love, no popular following. He was beaten, jailed, threatened, and even forced to leave his homeland. Only the pagan Babylonians showed him any respect (Jeremiah 39:11-12). God does not guarantee that serving him will get you public acclaim. But God does promise that he will be with you and give you strength to endure (2 Corinthians 1:3-7). As you minister to others, recognize that your service is for God, not for human approval. God rewards our faithfulness, but not always during our stay on earth.

♟ Tip for Parents

The more that kids know they are accepted and loved by their parents and the more they feel secure and connected at home, the less likely they will be to succumb to peer pressure like what Terri experienced in the story above. It's easier to endure loneliness outside the home if inside the home there is warmth and encouragement.

Loss

For some reason, a number of the families in Wynnwood Estates are undergoing real trials.

The Binns family is mourning the loss of Michelle's mother from a sudden heart attack. She was only fifty-six.

Last month the McGehee family suffered a devastating fire that destroyed most of the second floor of their home. Smoke and water damage took their toll on most of the contents of the first floor!

The Whitards are still reeling from the sudden layoff of Larry from his job. Like so many corporations, his is downsizing and streamlining its operations. Larry's severance package was decent, but at the age of forty-nine it's going to be difficult for him to find a comparable job with a comparable salary. A career counselor has warned that the family will probably have to relocate. To make matters worse, Larry and Sandy currently have two daughters attending a costly Christian college.

Anne Pearson is still trying to get back on her feet after having been deserted by her husband during the holidays. With three small children, she is wondering what the future holds—how she can support her kids financially and also give them the kind of emotional care they need.

○ Talk about It

- Which of the above situations would you personally find the most difficult? Why?
- How would you counsel the individuals in the story above? (That is, what would you say to give them comfort and hope?)
- What is the most difficult family situation you have ever encountered? Why?
- How have you been able to endure severe trials in life?

☑ Check It Out

Read Psalm 46:1-3 and note how it relates to the topic under discussion today.

♡ Apply It

The fear of mountains or cities suddenly crumbling into the sea as the result of a nuclear blast haunts many people today. But the psalmist says that even if the world ends, we need not fear. In the face of utter destruction, the writer expressed a quiet confidence in God's ability to save him. When you face an upheaval in your life that seems like the end of the world, the Bible is clear—God is our refuge even in the face of total destruction. He is not merely a temporary retreat; he is our eternal refuge and can provide strength in any circumstance. Do you ever feel that your life is too complex for God to understand? Remember, God created the entire universe, and nothing is too difficult for him. God created you; he is alive today, and his love is bigger than any problem you may face.

Tip for Parents

Two things are indispensable for surviving tough times in life: (1) a solid spiritual foundation and (2) close family ties. Expending time and energy to strengthen these areas even when times are good is like setting aside money for a rainy day—and when that day comes, you will be glad you planned for the future.

Love

The Lowe family is what you might call a model Christian family.

Mr. Lowe is a deacon and chairman of the missions committee. Mrs. Lowe teaches Sunday school and sings in the choir. The kids win awards every summer in Vacation Bible School—for both attendance and Scripture memory.

But that's just how they look when they're at church functions. You ought to see how they act at home.

Mr. Lowe routinely comes home from work and plops down in his La-Z-Boy recliner with the remote control—even on those nights when it's obvious Mrs. Lowe could use a little help corralling the kids and getting supper together.

And the kids fight like mortal enemies. Name-calling, arguing, tattling on each other—sometimes even throwing punches and other items with malicious intent!

How bad is it? Last night, *thirty seconds* after praying before dinner that God would "help us to be loving to each other," Tressa and her brother Benjamin got into an argument wherein Tressa snapped, "I hate you, you little twerp!"

◯ Talk about It

- Is love just a feeling? If not, what is it?
- Why is it so difficult sometimes to love the people in your own family?
- What does it say if a family is very involved in church or religious activities and yet they can't get along with each other?
- How would you feel if you were Mrs. Lowe and you had a husband and kids like hers?
- What are some ways your family fails to show love to one another?
- What are some loving things you could do for the people in your family this week?

☑ Check It Out

Measure your family's behavior this week against the checklist found in 1 Corinthians 13:4-7.

♡ Apply It

If our faith in Christ is real, it will prove itself at home, in our relationships with those who know us best. Children and parents have a responsibility to each other. Children should honor their parents even if their parents are demanding and unfair. Parents should care gently for their children even if the children are disobedient and unpleasant. Ideally, Christian parents and Christian children will relate to each other with thoughtfulness and love (Ephesians 6:1-4). This will happen if both parents and children put the others' interests above their own—that is, if they submit to one another.

♙♙ Tip for Parents

Help your children understand that love is more than mere emotion. (It is a commitment to seek good for others no matter what.) Help them understand the first part of 1 Corinthians 13—that if we fail to love, then all our good works (including our church activities) are meaningless. Help them to understand finally that loving others is impossible unless we are filled by the Spirit of God. Only with God's help are we capable of treating others the way God wants us to (Galatians 5:22-23).

Loyalty

When ten-year-old Kevin gets home from school, he's crying.

Joanne Andersen drops everything and runs over to comfort her sniffling son. "Honey, what's wrong?"

"This," he replies, handing his mom a folded-up piece of paper.

It is a note from his teacher that states that Kevin and some other kids were caught cheating on a spelling test. Due to their actions, the teacher has given each student a zero, and he wants to meet with each of their parents.

"You want to tell me about it?" Mrs. Andersen probes.

"I didn't cheat!" Kevin exclaims. "Pat and Charlie said I did, but I didn't."

"Why would they say that if it wasn't true?"

"I don't know. When Mr. Miller caught them whispering, Pat pointed at me and said I told him how to spell *application*. But I didn't. I swear I didn't cheat."

Mrs. Andersen looks her son in the eye and says, "I believe you."

Two days later, at an after-school conference, Kevin's teacher, Mr. Miller, presents some evidence that indicates Kevin may have, in fact, been guilty.

When she gets home, Joanne Andersen again questions her son. Again, he adamantly insists he is innocent.

Later that night Joanne asks her husband, Lee, "What are we supposed to believe?"

◌ Talk about It

- What does it mean to be loyal to someone?
- Parents, how do you feel when a child lies to you? Kids, how do you feel when you tell the truth and your parents don't believe you?
- Who would you believe in the situation just described? Why?

☑ Check It Out

Read 1 Corinthians 13:6-7 and relate it to your discussion of loyalty.

♡ Apply It

The Bible says that love protects, trusts, hopes, and perseveres. Love is of utmost importance. Love involves actions as well as attitudes. A loving person not only feels love; he or she also acts loyally and responsibly. A loving person not only believes the truth; he or she also works for justice for others. Thoughts and words are not enough—our lives reveal whether we are truly loving. Do your actions measure up to your attitudes?

▮▮ Tip for Parents

When your children do something to violate your trust, gradually give them the opportunity to regain that trust. It is important not to be blind to your children's faults, but it is equally important not to doubt them when they are being truthful.

Manipulation

It's Friday evening at the Dickinson residence, and there is a lot of manipulation going on. See for yourself:

- Stephanie is being very sweet and polite and helpful. She even set the table without being asked. Why? Because in a few minutes she plans to ask her mom if she can sleep over at a friend's house. Stephanie is supposed to be grounded, but she figures she can worm her way out of that by being extra nice.
- Stephen has already been told he can't go to the high school football game with another family. "You don't love me!" he moans. "Every single one of my friends is going to be there tonight. You're the only dad in town who won't let his son go to the games. How am I supposed to learn how to play football if I can't even go to the games?"
- Mr. Dickinson doesn't pay much attention to his son's comments. That's because he is thinking about how nice it would be to play golf at Oak Alley on Saturday morning. He's never played that course, but he keeps hearing from his friend Rick (a member!) how incredible it is. *Maybe if I called Rick and said, "Hey, I'm thinking about playing golf tomorrow at City Park. Wanna join me?" he'd ask me to play at Oak Alley!* With that thought he picks up the phone and starts dialing.

○ Talk about It

- What is manipulation? Why is it wrong?
- How is Stephanie being manipulative? What about Stephen? Mr. Dickinson?
- Instead of having hidden agendas, how should family members interact with each other?
- Is it wrong to want certain things? If not, why are the actions of the Dickinsons wrong?
- How do you feel when you sense that someone is manipulating you?

☑ Check It Out

The Bible counsels us to love each other, not to manipulate each other. See Romans 12:10 and John 13:34-35.

♡ Apply It

We're all selfish, and manipulating others is one way we try to get our way. Laban is a classic example—his whole life was marked by one attempt at manipulation after another (Genesis 24:1–31:55). He made arrangements for his sister Rebekah's marriage to Isaac so that he would profit, and he used his daughters' lives as bargaining chips. Jacob eventually outmaneuvered Laban, but the older man still tried to get Jacob to promise to be gone for good. He was always trying to get his way.

Don't be like Laban. Resist the urge to control people and events to your benefit. It's not right, and God will take care of you.

♟ Tip for Parents

It isn't just children who are manipulative. Parents quite commonly fall into the trap of trying to selfishly control their kids. Check your own habits and behavior today. Do you have a hidden agenda for your children? Are you trying to get them to do and be what *you* want, or are you primarily concerned that they please the Lord? There's a very subtle difference! Be up-front with your thoughts and feelings.

Memories

Ever since Judy Roberts went to a Memory Maker party, her family has been giving her grief. Suddenly she's a woman on a mission—to preserve their family pictures and mementos in very organized, very expensive scrapbooks.

Night after night she's been staying up late, cropping photographs, organizing memorabilia, and writing cute captions. "Mom," Sarabeth finally says, about two weeks into this massive project, "how long are you going to keep this up?"

"As long as it takes," Judy replies sweetly. "And you will thank me one day for this. Our whole family history will be preserved. You'll be able to hand this down to your children . . . and grandchildren."

Freddy is balancing the checkbook during this conversation. Without looking up he mumbles, "Will there be a page or two in there about how the family went bankrupt buying photo albums?"

Judy glances at him and says (for about the hundredth time), "Sweetheart, these materials cost more because they're acid-free and they won't damage our photos. What good would it do to go to all this trouble only to watch it all deteriorate in a few years?"

Freddy and Sarabeth look at each other and fight the urge to laugh.

○ Talk about It

- Why is it important to look back and remember the past?
- In addition to scrapbooks, what are some other ways families can preserve their histories?
- What has your family done with all its photos and mementos?
- How much do you know about your family background, genealogy, and history?
- What question about your family's past would you like to ask?
- How much are your memories worth to you? Could you set a dollar value on those moments?

☑ Check It Out

Consider how Joshua instructed the Israelites to preserve their special memories—Joshua 4:1-24.

♡ Apply It

When Joshua led the nation of Israel across the Jordan River, it was a historic moment. Joshua and the leaders therefore stopped and built a monument to commemorate the end of their wandering and the beginning of their new life in their new land (Joshua 4:2-7). While most monuments commemorate great events or acknowledge heroic deeds, individuals and families often keep mementos, photos, and other "monuments" to God's goodness—a special event, an answered prayer, a miracle. Though often less visible, these reminders are no less important than a big white statue. Think back over what God has done in your life. Let your memories serve as monuments, reminders of God's work in your life and of his care for you. And don't be ashamed of keeping physical pieces of these great events, commemoratives with infinite value.

👥 Tip for Parents

Three ideas for you: (1) Have a video-watching night or a slide-show night or a picture night in which you relive your family's past. (2) Make it a family project to trace your family tree. (3) Begin keeping a diary or journal that records answered prayers and other blessings from God. This can prove to be a continual source of encouragement for your whole family.

Money

Twelve-year-old Lance did odd jobs every chance he got this summer. He mowed and trimmed yards, he washed cars, he cleaned garages and attics—he even did a short stint as a dog walker.

In all, Lance earned $660. His parents are proud of his drive and determination. What has them concerned now is that Lance wants to go out and spend all his hard-earned money.

"Dad, have you seen the go-carts they have for sale at the lawn mower shop over on Georgia Street?"

"Yes, why do you ask?"

"Well, I was thinking about maybe using my money to get one. They—"

Lance's mom interrupts. "Oh no, you're not! No son of mine is going to kill himself in a miniature racing car!"

"Mom, they're not 'racing cars'! They go maybe thirty miles per hour."

"Well, I don't care if they only go ten miles per hour. You're not getting a go-cart."

"I don't see why I can't. It's my money. I earned it."

Lance's dad tries a different approach. "Son, maybe you ought to consider doing several different things with that money."

"What do you mean?"

"Well, you could put a big chunk of it in the bank. Then you'd have it later on—maybe to help you buy a real car. For now you could pick out one small thing you'd like to buy. . . . And, of course, there is always the issue of giving something back to God."

○ Talk about It

- Why is it easier to spend money than to save it or give it away?
- How much of what we earn should we give to God? Why?
- What are some ways that you waste money/could save money?

☑ Check It Out

Consider the messages of Proverbs 21:20 and Proverbs 22:9.

♡ Apply It

Easy credit has many people in our culture living on the edge of bank-ruptcy. The desire to keep up and to accumulate more pushes them to spend every penny they earn, and they stretch their credit to the limit. But anyone who spends all he has is spending more than he can afford. A wise person puts money aside for the future. God approves of foresight and restraint. We need to examine our lifestyle to see whether our spending is God-pleasing or merely self-pleasing.

♟ Tip for Parents

Make budgeting a family process. If you discuss God's ideas about money with your children, they will gain valuable understanding of an issue that causes the majority of people great heartache in life.

Motives

Seeing *what* people do is easy. Understanding *why* they do it is another story.

Take the Lumpkin family, for example.

Mr. Lumpkin is the nicest guy in the world. He never says no to anyone. He'll help you, do anything for you, even give you the proverbial shirt off his back. Often his helpfulness drives the rest of the family crazy. Why is he like this?

Mrs. Lumpkin is a cleaning machine. She keeps the Lumpkin home spotless. Not only is everything polished, it is also perfectly organized, stored, and labeled. Track dirt into her home, and within minutes it has vanished. Why is she such a neatnik?

Fifteen-year-old Ricky has a strange-looking haircut, and every couple of weeks or so he takes a box of gelatin and somehow uses it to temporarily "dye" his hair a different color. Why?

Eleven-year-old Randy plays basketball at least four hours a day. That's all he talks about or thinks about. Why?

○ Talk about It

- What are some of the unique behaviors of members of your family?
- Pick one of your behavioral traits, and think hard about it for a moment: *Why* do you think you do that thing?
- What are motives? Why are they significant?
- Give some possible explanations for the different actions of the members of the Lumpkin family.
- The last time you did something nice for someone, what was your real motive?
- What is your *real* motive for going to church?

☑ Check It Out

The Bible makes it clear that God not only takes note of our actions, he also knows (and cares deeply about) what our hidden motives are. Read 1 Chronicles 28:9; Proverbs 16:2; and 1 Corinthians 4:5.

♡ Apply It

It is easier to do what's right when we gain recognition and praise than when we get nothing for it. To be sure our motives are not selfish, we should do our good deeds quietly or in secret, with no thought of reward (Matthew 6:3-4). Jesus said we should check our motives whenever we give (6:4), pray (6:6), or fast (6:17-18). Those acts should come from a desire to please God, not to make us look good. The reward God promises has no weight, color, or cash value, and it never goes to those who seek it. Doing something only for a pat on the back is not a loving sacrifice. With your next good deed, ask, *Would I still do this if no one would ever know I did it?*

♛ Tip for Parents

In discussing motives, make sure your children understand that the point is not to try to second-guess others but to examine *their own hearts* before God. As in so many areas of life, our tendency is to play the psychologist or act as judge rather than focus on ourselves. Only God knows what motivates others. But with his help, we can realize what drives us.

Moving

Todd and his wife, Leanne, are discussing his job interview in Dallas.

"So, should we do it?"

Todd shrugs. "I don't know, hon. It seems like a great opportunity. I like the folks there. And I'd be making a lot more money. Plus I'd be doing the kind of work I'd really rather be doing."

"But what about moving to such a big city? Do we really want to do that?"

"I know, I know. I think about that. The crime, the traffic, a higher cost of living . . . but there would be some advantages, too."

"Like?"

"I don't know. More stores, better restaurants, more cultural advantages."

"Yeah, but what about all the stuff we'd be leaving—this house that we've worked so hard renovating . . . all our friends . . . our church?"

"They have churches in Dallas!"

"I know, but as good as ours? And what about the difference in the school systems? Here we know most of the teachers, and the school board is pretty conservative. There you have metal detectors and school-based clinics!"

"So how are we supposed to know what to do?"

Leanne shakes her head. "Don't ask me. I'm the one who can't stand the thought of change."

"Well, I'm supposed to give them an answer on Friday."

○ Talk about It

- If you could move or had to move anywhere else, where would you go? Why?
- If your family has recently experienced a move, what were the hardest parts about leaving your old place and the best parts about going to a new place?
- What factors should families consider before deciding to relocate?
- How much input should kids have in a family's decision to move?

☑ Check It Out

What help does James 1:5 give to those who face big decisions?

♡ Apply It

James is talking not only about knowledge but also about the ability to make wise decisions in difficult circumstances. Whenever we need wisdom, we can pray to God, and he will generously supply what we need. Christians don't have to grope around in the dark, hoping to stumble upon answers. We can ask for God's wisdom to guide our choices. *Wisdom* means practical discernment. It begins with respect for God, leads to right living, and results in increased ability to tell right from wrong. God is willing to give us this wisdom, but we will be unable to receive it if our goals are self-centered instead of God-centered. To learn God's will, we need to read his Word and ask him to show us how to obey it. Then we must do what he tells us.

♟ Tip for Parents

Conventional wisdom says that kids are tough and resilient, that they can quickly adapt to new surroundings. This is not always true. If you are considering a move, make a serious effort to find out what your kids are thinking and feeling.

Music

Jack and Suzanne Salter are suspicious when their eleven-year-old son comes walking in the door with a compact disc.

"What's that?"

"Just a CD I borrowed from Hunter."

"Who's it by?"

"S.T.P."

"S.T.P.? Hmmm, I never heard of that group. Are they new?"

"Sort of."

"What do the initials stand for?"

"I dunno. Sewage Treatment Plant or something like that."

"Ooooohhhh! That sounds kind of rough, Brent. And they look pretty wild, too. What kind of music do they play?"

"It's not too loud. I guess kind of alternative."

"Well, you know, Mom and I aren't familiar with that group. So I don't know—maybe you'd better let us look at that first and check it out. If it's OK, you can listen to it."

"Awww, Dad, nobody else's parents monitor their kids' music."

"Well, if that's true, that's a sad situation. Parents need to. Look, we just love you. And we don't want you putting a bunch of wrong ideas in your head."

"All right," Brent sighs as he heads up the stairs.

◯ Talk about It

- What is your favorite kind of music? song? CD? Why?
- Why do you think music networks such as MTV, VH-1, and CMT are so popular?
- Why do parents and children disagree so much about music?
- What's the most important issue in determining whether we should listen to a particular song—the kind of music, the song lyrics, or the lifestyle of the artist?
- Are Brent's parents wrong to monitor his music? Are they overreacting?

☑ Check It Out

Read Ephesians 5:8-19 and relate it to today's conversation about music.

♡ Apply It

Music played an important part in Israel's worship and celebration. Singing was an expression of love and thanks, and it was a creative way to pass down oral traditions. Some say the song of Moses recorded in Exodus 15:1-18 is the oldest song ever written down. It was a festive epic poem celebrating God's victory, lifting the hearts and voices of the people outward and upward. After having been delivered from great danger, they sang with joy. Psalms and hymns can be great ways to express relief, praise, and thanks. It is good and appropriate to celebrate God's goodness with music.

▮▮ Tip for Parents

There was a time not so long ago when young people laughed at the prospect of listening to so-called Christian music. It was called cheesy, amateurish, inferior, and worse. But times have changed. Christian artists now cover the spectrum and turn out quality products. Many parents have avoided the black hole of secular music by pointing their children toward quality contemporary Christian music.

Neighbors

Bill and Terrie Dorsey have a huge decision to make.

Because they live in a prime location along a major thoroughfare, an out-of-town developer has offered them big bucks for their home and property. He plans to have the land rezoned from residential to commercial. He then wants to build a huge shopping center there.

If Bill and Terrie sell, they stand to pocket more than a million dollars! They would be able to buy another home in any neighborhood in the city and still have lots of money left over.

However, because the Dorseys' property butts up against a beautiful old neighborhood, their decision will affect a number of other people. If they sell, their backyard neighbors (about five families) will end up living right next to a giant supermarket with twenty-four-hour traffic, big delivery trucks, a brightly lit parking lot, and big smelly Dumpsters.

"This is a once-in-a-lifetime opportunity for us," Terrie says one night as the family clears away the dinner dishes.

"Yeah, but all our neighbors will hate us if we sell," Bill notes.

"You should hear the kids on the bus!" twelve-year-old Seth exclaims. "All they talk about is whether we're going to sell!"

"What do they say?"

"That we're stupid if we don't take the money, and we're selfish if we do."

⟲ Talk about It

- What should the Dorseys do?
- What would you do in that situation?
- What factors should we consider when making a big decision like the one facing the Dorseys?
- What does it mean to "love your neighbor as yourself" (Luke 10:27)?

☑ Check It Out

Read Philippians 2:3-4 and consider how it might apply to situations like the one just described.

♡ Apply It

The Bible teaches that we are to lay aside selfishness and treat others with respect and common courtesy. Considering others' interests as more important than our own links us with Christ, who was a true example of humility.

Tip for Parents

As often as possible we need to challenge our children to see difficult situations from various perspectives. When they begin to feel or experience what others feel, they will be less likely to make selfish choices.

Obedience

Nobody in the Ducote family would even think of burglarizing a neighbor's home, shoplifting from a store, or taking the Lord's name in vain. All would quickly tell you they want to be obedient followers of Christ.

But consider the activities the Ducotes *do* regularly participate in:

Ronnie borrows music CDs from friends and makes tapes from them. His youth leader told him that this is illegal—that it violates copyright laws. Ronnie scoffs: "I'm not hurting anybody. Besides, these groups are making millions of dollars anyway!"

Before Ronnie's mom leaves fast-food restaurants, she often grabs fifteen to twenty extra packets of sweetener and a handful of plastic utensils. "That's why they're there," she rationalizes. "If they didn't want you to take them, they wouldn't leave them out like that."

Ronnie's brother (like everyone else where he works) arrives late and leaves a few minutes early. Lunch hours often stretch to an hour and a half. But are these lost minutes reflected in the time sheets Ronnie's brother turns in? No.

⟳ Talk about It

- What do you think about the habits of the Ducote family?
- What kind of testimony or witness do Christians have when they only partially obey the laws of God or the laws of men?
- In several places in the Gospels Jesus says that if we love him we will obey him. What would people say about your love for Jesus just from watching your life?
- What are some specific rules that you have a hard time obeying?
- How can family members encourage and help each other to be more obedient to Christ?

✉ Check It Out

Consider the words of Christ found in Luke 6:46 and John 14:23.

♡ Apply It

Numerous places in the Bible state the theme "to obey is better than sacrifice" (1 Samuel 15:22-23; Psalms 40:6-8; 51:16-17; Proverbs 21:3; Isaiah 1:11-17; Jeremiah 7:21-23; Hosea 6:6; Micah 6:6-8; Matthew 12:7; Mark 12:33; Hebrews 10:8-9). Does that mean that sacrifice is unimportant? Not at all. But God wants us to have the right reasons for making a sacrifice rather than merely going through a ritual. God doesn't care about the sacrifice alone because the sacrifice only demonstrates the relationship between the person and him. If the person doesn't really care about God and about obeying him, the sacrifice is a hollow ritual. "Being religious"—going to church, serving on a committee, giving to charity, praying, and the like—is not the heart of devotion to God. Consistent, faithful obedience to him is.

♟♟ Tip for Parents

Partial obedience is disobedience. Striving to be "mostly holy" is unholiness. Those who make it their goal "not to sin *too much*" are ignoring the fact that God wants complete submission. He wants us not to sin, period. If you are cutting ethical or moral corners in your life, be sure that your children will eventually catch on. And most likely, they will imitate your failure in the area of obedience.

Parents under Pressure

Because of pressures at work or concerns over her health or financial worries (or perhaps all three), Sarah's mom has been a grouch all week.

On Monday she made Sarah do the dishes (and it wasn't even her day).

On Tuesday she yelled at Sarah for leaving her bike out in the rain.

On Wednesday she made Sarah turn off the TV and study an extra thirty minutes.

On Thursday she made Sarah get off the phone and vacuum out the car.

On Friday she told Sarah she couldn't sleep over at a friend's house.

"I don't know what's up with my mom," Sarah complained to her friend, "but she's really acting weird lately. She jumps on me for everything I do and everything I say. I feel like I'm in prison and she's the warden!"

☿ Talk about It

- Why do you think parents sometimes get cranky?
- What do parents do that gets on kids' nerves?
- Why do parents make up so many rules?
- (For kids) Imagine being grown up and having your own family. In what ways will you be like your mom or dad? In what ways will you be different from them?
- What should children do if they disagree with something their parents ask them to do?

☑ Check It Out

Read what God expects of parents and children in Ephesians 6:1-4.

♡ Apply It

There is a difference between obeying parents and honoring them. To obey means to do what you're told; to honor means to show respect and love. God wants children to do both, as long it stays within God's law—he doesn't want us to disobey him in the process of obeying them. Obey *and* honor your parents while under their care. And after you grow up and leave home, always show honor to them. This is God's plan for everyone (Ephesians 6:1-2).

♟ Tip for Parents

Your children will be less likely to balk about family rules if they understand the reason behind each regulation. Let them know often of your desire to protect them (from bad situations, choices, and habits) and your goal to provide for them (the best, wisest, safest life possible). If they can see that the boundaries have been set with care and with their good in mind, perhaps they will be a little more agreeable. Nothing makes us madder than an arbitrary or unfair rule.

Parents Up in Front

The youth pastor at Hillsdale Community Church took a new position at another church last month. While the congregation searches for a new minister to students, the youth group members' parents are taking turns leading the meetings.

This Wednesday night it's Kristy Miller's dad's turn to teach the lesson—and the lesson is on *love.* Let's just say Kristy is not exactly thrilled.

When a friend asked her why she is so freaked out, Kristy responded, "You would have to know my dad. He always makes these really cheesy jokes, and . . . I don't know, he's sweet and everything, but he's my dad, for crying out loud! I just can't believe he's going to stand up there in front of the whole youth group and talk about love!"

When the meeting began on Wednesday night, Kristy could feel her heart pounding in her chest. She kept waiting for her dad to do something dumb.

But nothing embarrassing happened. In fact, when the discussion started, Mr. Miller got everyone talking and laughing. He made some really good points, and everyone felt it was one of the best youth meetings ever.

"Gosh, Kristy," several friends remarked afterwards, "we didn't know your dad was so cool!"

"Yeah, he's hilarious!"

Kristy isn't sure what to think. Are they talking about her dad?!

⟳ Talk about It

- Kids, how would you have felt in Kristy's situation?
- Parents, how would you have felt in Mr. Miller's situation?
- How can parents and children get past the kind of awkwardness described above and develop a warm relationship based on respect?
- Describe a way you have been "surprised" (in a good sense) by your parents.

☑ Check It Out

Read the command in Exodus 20:12.

♡ Apply It

The commandment to "honor your father and mother" is the first commandment with a promise attached. To live in peace for generations in the Promised Land, the Israelites would need to respect authority and build strong families. But what does it mean to "honor" parents? Partly, it means speaking well of them and politely to them. It also means acting in a way that shows them courtesy and respect. It means following their teaching and example of putting God first. Parents have a special place in God's sight. Even those who find it difficult to get along with their parents are still commanded to honor them. What are you doing to show respect to your parents? Are you living in a way that brings honor to them?

▮▮ Tip for Parents

Youth experts say that one of the worst mistakes an adult can make is to try to "act like a kid" in attempting to relate to young people. If you demonstrate interest and sincerity, kids will respect you, no matter what your age.

Parties

Driving Abby to a slumber party, her dad says to her, "Now, one more time, what are you going to do if everyone else wants to watch a video you don't need to be watching?"

"Daddy!"

"Ab, I just want you to be ready for whatever might happen."

"If they start watching some bad movie, I'll leave the room or I'll tell them I have to go home."

"OK."

After a few moments of silence, Abby says, "Daddy, why do you always worry so much about me when I leave?"

Mr. Wells reaches over and pats his daughter's knee. "Oh, baby, it's hard to explain. I just don't want you to get into situations where you feel out of control. I know you really want to do the right thing. And I'm so proud of you for that. But I also know that when all your friends are pressuring you, saying, 'C'mon! C'mon!' it's hard to remember what is right. And so I just try to get you prepared for whatever might come up."

"Oh."

In a few minutes, they reach the home where the party is being held. Abby grabs her bag and runs up the driveway. Then suddenly she spins and runs back to the car where her dad is waiting. Giving him a tight hug, she whispers, "I love you, Daddy."

"I love you, too. Use your head, OK? And have fun!"

"I will."

⟳ Talk about It

- What are the best and worst things about parties and/or sleepovers?
- Kids, how do you feel when your parents worry and fuss over you?
- Parents, why do you worry so much about your children?
- How come it is so difficult to remember what's right when all our friends are telling us to do what's wrong?
- Is it realistic to think that anyone would tell his or her friends, "If you are going to watch that movie, I'm going to have to leave"? Why or why not?

☑ Check It Out

How does Luke 23:13-25 relate to the subject at hand?

♡ Apply It

In Luke 23:13-25, we read that Pilate wanted to release Jesus, but the crowd loudly demanded his death; so Pilate sentenced Jesus to die. As a career politician, he knew the importance of compromise, and he saw Jesus more as a political threat than as a human being with rights and dignity. When the stakes are high, it is difficult to stand up for what is right, and it is easy to see our opponents as problems to be solved rather than as people to be respected. Had Pilate been a man of real courage, he would have released Jesus no matter what the consequences. But the crowd roared, and Pilate buckled. When we know what is right but decide not to do it, we are following Pilate's example. When you have a difficult decision to make, don't discount the effects of peer pressure. Realize beforehand that the right decision could have unpleasant consequences: social rejection, career derailment, public ridicule. Don't let circumstances or people's expectations control you. Be firm as you stand true to God, and refuse to compromise his standards for living.

♟ Tip for Parents

Write your child a note this week in which you express your love, support, and concern. It is a wonderful thing to feel cared for!

Peace

What's with the Adams sisters? For some reason they can't seem to get along today. Their first words this morning:

"Hey, turn out that light!"

"I've got to find my shoes!"

"Well, *I've* got to sleep, bonehead!"

"Girls!"

Then at breakfast:

"Hey, you ate all the Froot Loops!"

"There was only like *one bowl* left!"

"Liar! That's your second serving!"

"Girls!"

Then on the way to school:

"I get to sit up front."

"You did yesterday!"

"So, I called it first."

"So, I'm bigger than you."

"Yeah, you're big and *fat!*"

"Girls!"

Then after school:

"Get off the phone! Now!"

"You can't make me!"

"Wanna bet?"

"Mom! Jessica won't leave me alone!"

"Yeah, well *she's* been on the phone for about six hours!"

"Girls!"

⟳ Talk about It

- Do any of those scenes remind you of your family? Which ones? Why?
- What are some things that drive you crazy?
- Why is it so hard to get along with other people? Especially brothers and/or sisters?
- What are some things family members can do (specifically) to get along better and to avoid unnecessary conflict?
- Discuss your family's rules for name-calling and arguing.

☑ Check It Out

Compare Romans 12:18; Romans 14:19; and Colossians 3:15.

♡ Apply It

Moses once tried to negotiate and reason with the king of Edom but without success (Numbers 20:14-20). When nothing worked, he was left with two choices—force a conflict or avoid it. Moses knew there would be enough barriers in the days and months ahead. There was no point in adding another one unnecessarily. So he inconvenienced himself and his people to avoid a fight with Edom (20:21). Sometimes conflict is unavoidable, but often it isn't, and in many such cases the consequences of fighting far outweigh the benefits. Open warfare may seem heroic, courageous, and even righteous, but it is not always the best choice. Try hard to live at peace with everyone. Consider Moses' example, and find a peaceful way to solve your problems, even if it is hard to do.

Tip for Parents

Sometimes kids learn more when they are allowed to role-play. With that in mind, have your children act out the scenes above. Give them a scenario (maybe with some additional details), and instruct them to work at keeping the peace and resolving the conflict in a way that pleases God. They'll have fun, and the truth will sink in. For extra laughs, video their role-playing and show it to them.

Peer Pressure

On the way home from the police station, Dale's dad is quiet. Finally he says quietly, "Dale, I'm just shocked. That's all I can say. I'm just totally shocked."

Dale wishes his dad would yell or something. But he's unusually calm. It makes Dale feel even worse. He can't even make eye contact with his father.

"You are such a smart kid. You've got a good head on your shoulders. And you *know* what's right and what's wrong. That's why I just can't believe you would sit there and actually shoot your BB gun at cars!

"What were you thinking? Didn't your conscience say to you, 'Hey, Dale, this is wrong. This is stupid. You're gonna get in trouble'?"

Dale feels a big tear roll down his face. He's confused. The fact of the matter is that he *did* know that what he was doing was wrong. And he felt like running away. But his friends were laughing and urging him on.

"I'm sorry, Dad," Dale mumbles. "I guess I just wanted to be part of the gang."

⟳ Talk about It

- What is a *peer*?
- Define *peer pressure.*
- Why is peer pressure so strong?
- What are some ways you can feel your peers trying to influence you?
- Does peer pressure only push people to do *bad* things, or can it also cause people to avoid doing *good* things? Explain and/or give some examples.
- What is *positive* peer pressure?

☑ Check It Out

Read about the Jewish leaders who wanted to follow Jesus but wouldn't because of peer pressure—John 12:42-43.

♡ Apply It

Christians don't have to give in to public opinion and pressure because God loves us no matter what people think. The apostle Paul stood faithful to God whether people praised him or condemned him (2 Corinthians 6:8-10). He remained active, joyous, and content even under pressure. Don't let circumstances or people's expectations control you. Be firm as you stand true to God, and refuse to compromise his standards for living.

♟ Tip for Parents

A lot of Christian parents preach constantly against peer pressure but then resort to it when it serves their purpose. For example, Johnny doesn't want to eat vegetables at the church potluck, so Mom says, "Johnny, look over there at Susie. She's eating *her* vegetables!" This kind of manipulation sends mixed signals to our kids. Out of one side of our mouths we're saying, *"Don't* copy the behavior of your friends!" but out of the other side we're saying, *"Do* imitate others!" A better way is to teach our children to think, to evaluate for themselves (based on God's Word) whether a thing is true and right. If it is, we want them to do it, even if no one else does.

Persecution

The Simons have only been residents of Jonesboro for about a year, but in that time they have made a real effort to get to know their neighbors. It helps that they live on a cul-de-sac where almost every family has kids their age.

Over the last few months, a lot of the children have gravitated toward the Simons. Not only are their three children outgoing, but Lance and Rhonda also have a trampoline and a big backyard.

A few days ago when it was raining and the kids were whining, Rhonda stuck a video into the VCR for the kids to watch, but not just any video. It was a tape about the life of Jesus, and it concluded with a very straightforward appeal for children to "ask Jesus into their hearts" and then to go and "tell others to do the same thing."

Later on, Rhonda was thrilled when two little neighbors proudly announced that they had given their lives to Jesus. But she wasn't too excited that evening when she got an angry phone call from one of the girls' moms. And the Simons children were disappointed the next day when a couple of their best friends in the neighborhood said, "Our parents told us we can't come to your house anymore."

☼ Talk about It

- Look up the word *persecution* in the dictionary, and discuss its meaning.
- Did Mrs. Simon do anything wrong? Why or why not?
- Why did some of the moms and dads in the neighborhood get angry that their children had watched a video about Jesus?
- Have you ever had someone get mad at you or make fun of you for being a Christian?
- How does it feel to be teased or to be avoided because you are a follower of Jesus?
- What are some ways you can tell your friends about Jesus this week?

☑ Check It Out

Being persecuted because of our faith should not surprise us. See Matthew 10:22 and 2 Timothy 3:12.

♡ Apply It

In the days of the early church, Peter and John got in trouble for telling people about Jesus and inviting them to trust in him (Acts 5:40). Authorities warned them repeatedly not to preach. Still, they continued in spite of the threats. Their duty to speak went further than the Pharisees' preference that they stay silent. You may not be beaten or thrown in jail for speaking about Christ, but you may be ridiculed, ostracized, or slandered. As long as you have been gentle and respectful in your delivery, don't let such opposition deter you from sharing your faith.

👥 Tip for Parents

Be bold with the gospel, but be careful not to be sneaky about proselytizing your children's friends. Let other parents know beforehand that you are planning to show a video or sponsor a Backyard Bible Club. That way, they can decide if they want their child to participate. By being up-front, you may even get an opportunity to share your faith with a parent!

Plans

Friday night is always family night at the Wheelers'. They set aside this special night for doing all kinds of fun activities together. Sometimes they make their very own pizzas. Other times they put up the tent in the living room (or even in the backyard) and camp out. One Friday, Christy scavenged a bunch of appliance boxes. Then that night, with a big roll of duct tape and a box cutter, she and David created a cool maze for Hannah to crawl around in.

This week the plans are *really* exciting. They're going to meet the McGehee family at a local elementary school for Spring Fling—a fun carnival featuring all kinds of games and special events. Hannah has been so excited for the last few days that she can hardly stand it.

On Friday evening, just as the Wheelers are finishing dinner and preparing to drive over to Glenview School, the phone rings.

It's David's sister on the phone, and she's crying. Her sixteen-year-old son has just been in a car wreck. He's undergoing emergency surgery at a hospital thirty-five miles away.

Hannah watches as her parents confer in worried tones. She doesn't understand everything they're saying, but she can tell something bad has happened.

"Are we still going to go to Spring Fling?" she finally asks.

"No, honey," Christy replies, "I'm afraid we have to change our plans. Your cousin Mark is at the hospital, and he's hurt very badly. We need to drive to Monroe."

"But you and Daddy promised!"

"I know, sweetie. But Aunt Jeannie needs us. She's really sad."

"Well, now *I'm* sad, too! And I'm also *angry!*"

⟳ Talk about It

- What do you think about the Wheelers' tradition of family night?
- Why is Hannah so upset?
- How do you feel when your plans get messed up? Why?
- Is it wrong for Hannah to feel sad and angry? Why?
- How could Hannah make the best of this situation?

☑ Check It Out

Read Mark 6:30-34 for an example of how Jesus responded when his plans for a private retreat went awry.

♡ Apply It

It is good to have goals, but goals will disappoint us if we leave God out of them. There is no point in making plans as though God does not exist, because the future is in his hands (James 4:13-16). What would you like to be doing ten years from now? one year from now? tomorrow? How will you react when God steps in and rearranges your plans? Plan ahead, but hold your plans loosely. Put God's desires at the center of your planning; he has better plans anyway.

▐▌ Tip for Parents

If you don't already do it, consider instituting a family night in your home. This can become a cherished tradition that builds a lot of positive family memories.

Prayer
RITUALS

The Melton family sits down at the dinner table, and Dad says, "Who would like to say the blessing?"

Nobody responds for several seconds until finally six-year-old Andy says rather reluctantly, "I'll do it." Then he proceeds to say the exact same prayer he's been saying for the last year. It goes like this:

"Dear God, thanks for our food, thanks for our family, thanks for all you do, in Jesus' name, amen."

He says it in robotic fashion—quickly and with no feeling or expression. And then the family begins to grab for rolls and butter, and Andy and his little brother start fighting over who gets the drumsticks.

⟳ Talk about It

- Why do we pray before meals?
- What exactly is prayer?
- Why is prayer necessary? Or is it?
- What is the difference between saying prayers in ritualistic fashion and praying in a conversational manner?
- How do you think God feels when we just say a mindless, unfeeling prayer?
- Besides meals, when does your family pray together?

☑ Check It Out

Read what Jesus said about prayer in Matthew 6:5-15.

♡ Apply It

Repeating the same words over and over like a magic incantation is no way to ensure that God will enjoy your prayer. It's not wrong to come to God many times with the same requests—Jesus encourages *persistent* prayer. But he condemns the shallow repetition of words that come from an insincere heart (Matthew 6:7-8). We can never pray too much if our prayers are honest and sincere. Before you start to pray, make sure you mean what you say.

▮▮ Tip for Parents

If we pray only before meals, then our children will get the twisted idea that prayer is only a ritual to be used at specific times and specific places. By praying at all times (1 Thessalonians 5:17)—in the car, on a walk, for a sick pet, etc.—we send the powerful message that prayer is an ongoing conversation with God. Few lessons are as important as that one.

Prayer
EFFECTIVENESS

What's wrong with this scenario?

The Hunters are wrestling with and debating the merits of a new job offer that would mean a large increase in income but also a possible move. After dinner they're arguing about the pros and cons of starting all over in a bigger city.

Things get pretty emotional and personal. Jerry, who is practically drooling over the thought of a big pay increase, snaps at his wife, Stacey, for dragging her feet. Hurt and angry, and with a lot of resentment that has built up over the last few months, she snaps right back.

Daughter Cynthia objects tearfully to the whole idea. She can't stand the thought of moving away from her boyfriend, Robert. Lately she has let their physical relationship get a little bit out of control, but she couldn't bear the thought of losing him. And now Dad is talking about moving away!

"Well," Jerry finally snarls, "I guess discussing this is getting us nowhere. Let's pray about it." Reluctantly the family members bow their heads and begin fumbling for words to say to God.

○ Talk about It

- Do your prayers ever seem to bounce off the ceiling? When? Why?
- How important is our "heart condition" when we pray? Why?
- Does God hear all our prayers? Are there ever times when he turns a deaf ear to our requests?
- What are some issues or conditions that can hinder our prayers?
- What is wrong with Jerry's attitude? Stacey's? Cynthia's?
- What needs to change in your life so that your prayers are pleasing to God and not offensive to him?

☑ Check It Out

Read about some obstacles to prayer in Psalm 66:18; James 4:3; Proverbs 21:13; 1 Peter 3:7; Mark 11:25; and James 1:5-7.

♡ Apply It

Anger and strife make praying difficult (1 Timothy 2:8). That is why Jesus said we should interrupt our prayers, if necessary, to make peace with others (Matthew 5:23-24). God wants us to pray, but not at the expense of our relationships with each other. It's a matter of priorities—we must make time for reconciliation above almost everything else, including prayer. Pray under the right conditions: Make it your goal to have a right relationship with others so you are always free to pray.

♟♟ Tip for Parents

Many Christians find it helpful to pray along the lines of the acronym C-A-T-S. The *C* stands for *confession*; *A* for *adoration*; *T* for *thanksgiving*; and *S* for *supplication*. Confession comes first because it is important to make sure that we do not have any unconfessed sin in our lives. God is holy, and we must not think we can approach him if we are consciously living in a way that is not pleasing to him.

Prayer
ANSWERS

Christa is having some doubts about prayer.

"I guess sometimes I feel like my prayers fall on deaf ears. Or like some people say, 'They just bounce off the ceiling.' I mean, if God already knows everything, then why take the time to stop and pray? And if he's in control of everything that happens—if things are predestined to happen—then I wonder, *How is this prayer going to change anything?*

"And then there's this: There are millions of Christians all over the world. And they're all talking to God. It's hard to understand how God can hear them all, much less answer all those requests. I just wish prayer could be more personal. I wish I could feel like God was really sitting there listening to me.

"I feel bad that I have these thoughts. I guess I should just have more faith. But if I'm honest, that's how I feel."

↻ Talk about It

- What's the best answer to prayer you have ever received?
- Do you ever feel like Christa? Why or why not?
- Does prayer really change things? How do you know?
- If God does already know what we think, why should we pray?
- How do you think God can hear all his children praying at the same time?
- What is something you'd like to pray about right now?

☑ Check It Out

The Scriptures reveal that God *loves* to hear us pray (Proverbs 15:8) and that he delights to answer our requests (Matthew 7:11). Did you know that God is even available to help us pray (Romans 8:26)?

♡ Apply It

Jesus used the expression "you sinful people" to contrast sinful and fallible human beings with the holy and perfect God (Matthew 7:11). Christ is showing us the heart of God the Father. God is not selfish, begrudging, or stingy, and we don't have to beg or grovel as we come with our requests. He is a loving Father who understands, cares, and comforts. If people can be kind, imagine how kind God, the Creator of kindness, can be.

▮▮ Tip for Parents

This tip bears repeating: Keep a family notebook or journal of answered prayers. Such a record catalogs God's goodness and faithfulness and thereby serves as a great encouragement to your family to keep praying and trusting. Simply make three columns: Requests; When First Made; When Answered. Things really get exciting when you fill up the first notebook and have to start volume 2!

Prejudice

Carol Martin was excited to get an invitation to join the local Ladies' League. Not only does the group provide a lot of social interaction, but its members band together for some very worthwhile service projects in the community.

After being in the group for six months, Carol earned the right to nominate someone else for membership. Without hestitation, Carol submitted in writing the name of her friend Maria Hernandez. Later that day, the phone rang. It was the secretary of the Ladies' League calling to tell Carol that Maria's nomination would probably not be accepted.

"Why? Is something wrong?"

"Well . . . ," was the nervous, awkward reply, "it's hard to explain, really. I guess it's just that nobody really knows Maria—"

"I know her."

"Well, yes. But she's only lived here for about a year."

"So? You asked me to be in L. L. when I had only lived here for four months."

"Well, that was a different situation."

"How?"

"Carol, look. I didn't want to have to be so blunt, but you leave me no choice. There's a *huge* cultural and socioeconomic difference between Maria and the rest of the women in the group. It just wouldn't be a good idea."

Carol could not believe what she was hearing, and she was furious. "Missy, you know what? I'm going to go tell Maria that she's too good for your little club. Oh, and by the way, you can announce my resignation at the next meeting."

♻ Talk about It

- What is racial prejudice? What causes it?
- Do you think Carol overreacted? If so, why?
- What would you do in a similar situation?
- How does racial prejudice show itself in the town or city where you live?
- What do you think Jesus would say to people like Missy and clubs like the Ladies' League?

☑ Check It Out

Read about how Christ can break down the barriers that separate people who are different—Galatians 3:26-28 and Ephesians 2:11-18.

♡ Apply It

All people are related, going back to Adam and Eve. Humankind is a family that shares one flesh and blood. Remember this whenever racial prejudice enters your mind or hatred invades your feelings. Each person is a valuable and unique creation of God. No one matters less or deserves second-class treatment merely because of racial or ethnic identity.

♟♟ Tip for Parents

Get the text of Martin Luther King Jr.'s "I Have a Dream" speech. Have someone in your family read it, and then discuss it. Even better, see if you can get a copy of it on tape. The speech is sprinkled with biblical allusions and talks about true brotherhood in Christ.

Presumption

A couple of years ago, the Clays instituted a family council. They set aside the first Sunday night of each month to talk about problems and plans as well as to "get on the same page" schedulewise. It's been a very helpful practice. Holding these regular family forums has significantly helped the Clays (all five of them) with their communication and has sharpened their conflict-resolution skills.

Last night at the family council, when it was his turn to speak, Scott outlined some very detailed and ambitious educational goals for his girls. Then he discussed his strong desire to build a new home within three years. (Important background note: In the last couple of months, Scott Clay has been singled out for a possible advancement—and big pay raise—at work. He's practically been salivating at how such a promotion would help the family financially.)

Veronica listened to Scott politely and then said, "Scott, I think those are *great* plans, I really do. I want to see the girls go to good colleges. And I wouldn't mind building our dream house either. But how in the world are we going to be able to do those kinds of expensive things on your salary?"

"Have you forgotten my promotion?"

"Scott, you haven't been promoted yet!"

"Yeah, but the word is, it's just a matter of time. It's gonna happen. Everybody's saying that."

"Do you think maybe you're jumping the gun a little bit?"

"Veronica!"

✪ Talk about It

- What are some plans you like to accomplish individually? As a family?
- How do you feel when your plans fall through?
- What is the difference between planning for the future and presuming on the future?
- Was Veronica being mean or insensitive to question his plans?
- What does it mean to trust God with your future?

☑ Check It Out

See what God says about presuming upon the future in James 4:13-16.

♡ Apply It

Everyone has expectations for the future, but the future rarely happens the way we expect. We must make our predictions about it with humility, realizing that it all belongs to God and may be radically different from what we think (James 4:13-16). Whatever you assume about your future—whether ten years or ten minutes from now—do not presume upon it. Wait for the future to arrive before stating what you will do with it. Live today with what you have today, not with what you expect to have someday. Today has enough trouble of its own (Matthew 6:34).

❙❙ Tip for Parents

If you are careful not to get too carried away, it can be a helpful exercise to sit down with your family quarterly (or annually, at the very least) and discuss plans and goals. One family, recognizing the fleeting nature of time, came up with a list of six vacations they would like to take before their kids graduate from high school and leave home. Having such a list gives them direction and enables them to plan and save far in advance.

Priorities

There they are, just like every week, sitting in the third pew on the right side of the sanctuary—the six members of the Martin family.

Look at them. They're paying careful attention to the sermon on "Loving God with All Your Heart." Right? Wrong. They're distracted. Their thoughts are elsewhere. Each one is in his or her own little world.

Pam, six, is drawing a picture of Disney's Little Mermaid. And she's thinking about swimming and jumping off the diving board.

Peter, nine, is staring at the choir loft, but he's daydreaming about baseball. In his mind he's replaying all the home runs he saw on *SportsCenter* last night. *What if I hit a home run in my game tomorrow night?* he thinks. Suddenly he's smiling.

Patricia, thirteen, is writing the name *Kyle* all over her bulletin. That's her new boyfriend.

Paula, fifteen, is looking down at her arms and thinking, *My tan is nonexistent. I've got to lay out today.*

Mr. Martin's mind is wandering, too. A remark about money in the sermon has him thinking about whether to move the money from his bond fund into a more aggressive stock fund.

Mrs. Martin finds herself making a mental checklist of all the activities this week. *Between ball practices, swim team, youth group meetings, and birthday parties, I'm going to be in the van four hours a day!*

○ Talk about It

- What does it mean when we talk about our priorities?
- How can we determine what a person's priorities are?
- What kinds of things do you think about and daydream about? How come?
- Is it *wrong* for the Martin family members to be involved in the activities described above? Why or why not?
- Is it possible to have good priorities but have them arranged in the wrong order?
- Where does God fit into your priorities? Do you make time for him? Compared to everything else in life, where does getting to know him and serving him fall on your list of "things that are important to me"?

✉ Check It Out

Read Deuteronomy 6:5 and Colossians 1:18 and discuss what they have to say about the subject of priorities.

♡ Apply It

Many people claim to know God, but who really does? Priorities tell a lot of the story (Titus 1:16). Priorities determine many lifestyle choices, which then reflect what we value and whether we have ordered our lives around kingdom priorities. In other words, our conduct speaks volumes about what we believe (1 John 2:4-6). What do people know about God and about your faith by watching your life? If you know God, making good choices will never be easy, but it will be important to you, and that will drive you to make them.

Tip for Parents

It's fairly easy to determine what your true priorities are. Look at how you spend your time. Consider what you think about (and dream about) when your mind is unoccupied. Evaluate how you spend your money. It's a good exercise to take some time every week to ask ourselves (and our family members), "What are we living for?" and "What are we giving our lives to?" If we do not actively choose the best priorities, we will end up being involved in unworthy pursuits.

Privacy

It's wash day, and Sonya Dutton is sorting clothes and going through pockets.

In her daughter Sharon's khakis, she finds a five-dollar bill. In her son Austin's pants, she finds a folded-up piece of paper.

If this is another note from his teacher, Sonya silently threatens, *he is in big trouble!* Unfolding it, she sees a teenage boy's handwriting. She begins to fold the note back together when, out of the corner of her eye, she spies a dirty word that causes her to do a double take.

Looking closer at the note, she discovers more than just a dirty word or two—her son and his best friend, Andrew, are planning to sneak out on Friday night. The note mentions going "over to Christa's 'cuz her parents won't be home!"

Sonya is standing in the driveway with the note in hand when Austin gets home from school.

"You want to explain this?" she snaps.

Austin immediately gets defensive. He responds with a mixture of irritation and sheepishness. "Hey, where'd you get that?"

"Never mind where I got it. . . . The fact is, I do have it. You're not going anywhere Friday night. I can't believe you would lie to your dad and me!"

"I can't believe you would go snooping through my stuff!"

"Well, we'll talk about that when your dad gets home. For now, go to your room!"

⟳ Talk about It

- Was it wrong for Mrs. Dutton to read her son's note? Why or why not?
- Why is it important for individuals to have a certain amount of privacy?
- What is the difference, if anything, between privacy and secrecy?
- What factors in your home make privacy a rarity?

☑ Check It Out

Read 1 Corinthians 13:4-7 and Hebrews 4:13.

♡ Apply It

Nothing can be hidden from God. He knows about everyone everywhere, and everything about us is wide open to his all-seeing eyes. God sees all we do and knows all we think. Even when we are unaware of his presence, he is there. When we try to hide from him, he sees us. We can have no secrets from God. This should make us careful about what we do and say "in secret." We can also be comforted in realizing that although God knows us intimately, he still loves us.

👥 Tip for Parents

A good rule of thumb is this: The older children become, the more privacy they will both need and desire. Consequently, we need to work hard when kids are young to establish good communication habits that will enable us to survive (and even thrive) in the difficult growing years.

Pure Thoughts

It's hard to stay pure in a world that's morally impure.

If you don't believe that, just ask any member of the Woessner family.

Mr. Woessner is a bona fide Net surfer. With his home computer, he's hooked up to the information superhighway. How convenient to be able to E-mail friends in seconds! How great to have access to so much helpful information via the World Wide Web! How dangerous to be able to access hard-core electronic pornography at the touch of a few buttons!

Randy Woessner, thirteen, has a friend in the neighborhood who's hooked up to hundreds of TV channels (including all the nasty ones) via a satellite dish.

Even ten-year-old Steven Woessner is wrestling with the whole purity issue. Magazines (like the *Sports Illustrated* swimsuit issue) and catalogs (like *Victoria's Secret*) arrive in the family mailbox on a regular basis. And some of the billboards on the highway near his home are pretty provocative, too.

⟳ Talk about It

- Why is our world so obsessed with sexuality and the human body?
- Discuss this statement: "Naked bodies and sex were designed by God; therefore, there is nothing sinful about them."
- Why do guys seem to struggle more than girls with impure thoughts and temptations to lust?
- How can families guard against pornography and sexually oriented material?
- What does your family need to change this week about the way it uses the media (magazines, books, on-line services, television, etc.)?

☑ Check It Out

Read three passages that challenge us to be pure in our thinking: Psalm 119:9; Matthew 5:27-28; and Philippians 4:8.

♡ Apply It

Everywhere we look we find temptation to lead impure lives. The psalmist asked a question that troubles us all: How do we stay pure in a filthy environment (Psalm 119:9)? We cannot do this on our own but must have counsel and strength more dynamic than the tempting influences around us. How can we find that strength and wisdom? By reading God's Word and doing what it says.

👥 Tip for Parents

Never before have parents faced so many challenges in raising morally pure kids. Sexually explicit and suggestive materials are everywhere. Our culture bombards us with indecent words and images. We can either go on the defensive and constantly react and respond to these attacks, or we can take the offensive and be preemptive in our training. The latter course of action is wiser. Rather than trying to deprogram your kids, it is better to give them a solid foundation and starting point—i.e., a Christian perspective on sex. Teach them what God says, and show them how to think for themselves. They're going to hear it all from somebody. Surely they need to hear it first from godly parents.

Racism

For the last week it has been the focus of talk shows, newscasts, and dinner conversations. It's this week's cover story in almost every major news magazine.

"It" is yet another shocking videotape recording—this time of police beating a young Asian man. The man is a known gang member and is the leading suspect in the ambush of a police officer.

Central to the debate is the ever-present issue of racism. Was the man beaten because he is a member of a minority? Or was he treated roughly because he violently resisted arrest?

The police are claiming that the man was a threat, that the officers were only attempting to defend themselves. The Asian community feels that the arresting officers (three whites and one Hispanic) used excessive force merely because of the man's ethnic identity.

The Ramsay family discusses the case at dinner.

"Why is it that every time anything happens, somebody screams, 'Racism!'?"

"I don't know, but you have to admit that racism *is* a problem in this country."

"Well, maybe so, but is it possible that their screaming about it all the time only makes the problem worse?"

"Maybe so. But you might feel differently if *you* were a minority."

☾ Talk about It

- How would you define *racism*?
- What instances of racism have you personally witnessed? How did you feel when you observed these attitudes or actions?
- What do you think causes people of different races to mistrust each other?
- What, if anything, could be done to diminish racial prejudice in this country?
- Do you think you are a racist? Why or why not?

☑ Check It Out

How do the truths presented in Genesis 1:26-27 and Galatians 3:26-28 contribute to this discussion about racism?

♡ Apply It

In New Testament times, some Jewish males greeted each new day by praying, "Lord, I thank you that I am not a Gentile, a slave, or a woman." Christ taught his followers to have a new kind of attitude toward people who differed from them—an attitude of love and acceptance. Faith in Christ transcends differences in race, social standing, sex, and position and makes all believers one in Christ (Galatians 3:28). Make sure you do not impose distinctions that Christ has removed. Because all believers are his heirs, no one is more privileged than or superior to anyone else.

Tip for Parents

One family combats racial prejudice by devoting one night a week to learning about other cultures. Sometimes they dress up in native garb. Sometimes they read encyclopedias about another country or take a video tour (using tapes from the local library). Always they cook and sample recipes that are popular in the country they are studying. Not only does this weekly event provide a good time of family interaction, but the children learn to appreciate those who are different.

Regrets

Today is the day that Adam had been looking forward to for three weeks. Today is the Little League Baseball championship game—the Cubs vs. the Braves. Adam is supposed to be the Cubs' starting pitcher. But he won't be playing in the biggest game of his life. In fact, he won't even get to attend the game. Why?

Two days ago, Adam and his friend Michael were messing around in an old, abandoned house in the woods behind Michael's house. They shouldn't have been there, and they knew it. Not only were No Trespassing signs all over the place, but Michael's mom had specifically told them not to go near the house. "I don't want y'all playing back there," she warned. "That place is condemned. It's not safe."

Well, the boys didn't listen. And while they were messing around up in the attic, the rafters gave way. The boys fell about twelve feet. Michael ended up with thirteen stitches. Adam ended up with a severely shattered pitching arm. He'll be in the hospital another three days.

☯ Talk about It

- What's the reason Adam is missing out on the big game?
- What are some past decisions you regret?
- What are some ways we can avoid having regrets or avoid having to endure painful consequences?
- What would you tell Adam if he asked you, "Why did this have to happen to me?"
- What are some big decisions you are facing this week?

✉ Check It Out

Read about what happened to the Israelites when they regretted disobeying God and then tried to pretend they would be unaffected by the consequences—Numbers 14:40-45.

♡ Apply It

Esau's story shows us that mistakes and sins sometimes have lasting consequences (Genesis 25:29-34; 27:36). Even repentance and forgiveness do not always save us from the consequences of a bad choice. How often do you make decisions based on what you want now rather than on what you need in the long run (Hebrews 12:16-17)? Evaluate the long-range effects of your decisions and actions before you make them.

👫 Tip for Parents

We live in a culture where kids are taught to live for the moment. All that matters is today. Do whatever you want, and don't worry about tomorrow. The effect of this kind of existential philosophy is that kids fail to see connections between present behavior and future consequences. We can give our children a great gift if we drive home for them the truth that "what you do today plays a huge part in what you will experience tomorrow." That's a constant theme of the Scriptures. Wise people plan ahead. Fools do whatever seems right at the moment.

Reputation

Scott walks into his new fourth-grade class, and Mrs. Shiflet greets him with this statement:

"So *you're* Scott. Well, it's good to finally meet you. I've heard a lot about you."

"Ma'am?"

"I said, 'I've heard a lot about you.'"

Scott's face flushes as he looks down at the floor. "Um, yeah . . . Bad stuff, huh?"

"Some."

"Oh."

"But you know what?"

"What?"

"I don't believe a word of it."

Scott looks up, surprised. "You don't?"

"No, I don't. It doesn't matter to me what people say. And I don't care what happened in the past. This is a new year. We all get to start over."

"Yes, ma'am."

"Scott, let's make a deal."

"What kind of deal?"

"A secret deal where you and I show everybody else at school—all the other teachers—that everything they say about you is wrong. Let's show them how smart you are and how well you can behave."

Scott's smile gets broader and broader as he ponders that offer.

"OK," he says, nodding. "OK!"

♻ Talk about It

- What is a reputation?
- How do we get our reputations?
- What can we do if we have a bad reputation? How do we fix it?
- What kind of reputation would you like to have? In other words, when people mention your name, what kinds of things do you want them to think about you?
- How does your reputation affect God's reputation?

✉ Check It Out

Note what King Solomon said about maintaining a good reputation in Proverbs 22:1 and Ecclesiastes 7:1.

♡ Apply It

No wonder Boaz noticed Ruth—she was easy to admire. She was hardworking, loving, kind, faithful, and brave (Ruth 2:10-12). These qualities gained for her a good reputation because she displayed them *consistently* in all areas of her life. Wherever Ruth went or whatever she did, her character shone through.

Your reputation is formed by the people who watch you at work, in town, at home, in church, and on your way to and from each of these areas of your life. A good reputation comes from consistently living in imitation of Christ—no matter what group of people or circumstances surround you. Let your reputation speak for itself.

♟ Tip for Parents

While reputation matters a lot, character is far more important. Help your children understand that reputation is what others think them to be, while character is what they really are. Generally speaking, a person of character will have a good reputation. However, it is possible to possess a good reputation and yet lack character. Concentrate on consistently doing what is right. This is the way to build both a solid character and a respected reputation.

Reunions

Samantha just went from the mountaintop of joy to the valley of despair in about thirty seconds.

Her friend Jennifer just invited her to a waterskiing party. When Sam hung up, her mom asked, "What day is Jennifer's party?"

"The ninth of June."

"Oh no, Sam. I was afraid of that."

"Afraid of what?"

"Well, that's the weekend of Aunt Marge and Uncle Jim's fiftieth wedding anniversary."

"So?"

"So, we've made plans to go—the whole family. In fact, it's kind of turned into a family reunion."

"Aw, Mom, can't you and Dad go by yourselves . . . and let me stay here and go to Jennifer's thing? I'm almost fifteen."

"Sam, this is a big deal for Aunt Marge. And besides, you haven't seen some of your relatives in years. Who knows when you'll get to see them again? No, you need to call Jennifer back and tell her that you'll ski with her another time."

"But, Mom, who says there's going to be a next time? This is a really important party. C'mon, Mom!"

"No, dear. I want you to come with us."

"But I could stay with Stephanie. She's going to the party."

"Sam, it's decided. You're coming with us to the reunion. Let's drop it, OK?"

◯ Talk about It

- Have you ever had a family reunion? Would you like to have one (or have another one)?
- Which of your relatives do you enjoy being around the most and why?
- What are some good things that can happen at family reunions?
- If Samantha came to you for advice, what would you say to her?

☑ Check It Out

Note that the Year of Jubilee was intended to be a giant family reunion—Leviticus 25:10. Then with your family, scan the first eight chapters of the book of 1 Chronicles.

♡ Apply It

The record of names recorded in several chapters of 1 Chronicles is the official family record of the nation of Israel. It gives an overview of the history of God's work from Creation through the captivity of his people, tracing the roots of the nation from Adam onward, recounting its royal line and the loving plan of a personal God. The record served to teach the exiles returning from Babylon about their spiritual heritage as a nation and to inspire them to renew their faithfulness to God. Although these lists show the racial heritage of the Jews, they contain the spiritual heritage for every believer. We are a part of the community of faith that has existed from generation to generation.

Knowing our own family line and the heritage from which we came gives us an appreciation for the interworkings of families, the common roots, the shared genetic traits, and the warm traditions. We can also appreciate the greater family of God that draws together people from all different races, backgrounds, and nations to be in his family and to share with him at last in his Kingdom.

♟ Tip for Parents

It's often difficult to get scattered families together for reunions; so consider making a home video to send to relatives you haven't seen in a while. Done right, it can really be a fun family project!

Revenge

Ross, age nine, has been working in his room for several days on a giant Lego building project—a castle complete with a moat, drawbridge, several towers, and even a dungeon.

Moments ago, after watching a TV program about tornadoes, four-year-old Troy rumbled through the house, spinning as he went, saying, "Look at me! I'm a giant twister!"

You probably don't have to think too hard to figure out what happened next. Troy, the human tornado, encountered Ross's Lego castle. The castle didn't stand a chance.

"Troy! Noooo! Mom! Troy wrecked my castle!" Ross screams through real tears. *"It's ruined!"* Then, with anger flashing in his eyes, Ross grabs his little brother and starts punching him. *"Ahhhhh!"*

Mrs. Milligan steps in. "Ross, let go of your little brother!"

"But, Mom, look at what he did!"

"I'll deal with him."

"Yeah, well, *I'll* deal with him, too!"

"No, you won't. You keep your hands to yourself."

"Well, I'm gonna go into his room and tear up something that's his!"

"Don't you dare!"

"Why not? He did it to me!"

"That doesn't mean you do it back."

○ Talk about It

- What is revenge? When do you feel like getting revenge?
- Is it wrong to want revenge? Why or why not?
- How is revenge different than punishment?
- How would you feel if you were Ross?
- What should happen to Troy?
- Instead of taking revenge, how should Christians act when they have been mistreated?

☑ Check It Out

God says that we are to leave vengeance to him. See Romans 12:19-21.

♡ Apply It

When we are wronged, often our first reaction is to get even. But Jesus said we should do *good* to those who wrong us (Matthew 5:38-42). Our desire should be not to keep score but to love and forgive. This is not natural, it is supernatural. Only God can give us the strength to love as he does. Instead of planning vengeance, pray for those who hurt you.

▮▮ Tip for Parents

The desire for vengeance is really nothing more than a desire for justice. Kids who know that their parents are fair and impartial feel less of a need to "pay back" brothers and sisters. At the same time, we need to make sure our children understand that life isn't fair. There will be times when we are mistreated and no justice is administered, at least in this life. Even in those circumstances, we are not to be vigilantes who seek to dole out retribution.

Sacrifice

"Scott, have you packed your suitcase yet?"

"Suitcase? Why do I need a suitcase?"

"Because we're leaving for Grandma's as soon as your dad gets home."

"Huh?"

"Scott! Where have you been the last week? Don't you remember? It's Grandma's sixty-fifth birthday tomorrow. We're joining Aunt Linda and her family and Uncle Pete and his family and throwing Grandma a big surprise party. Remember?"

"But, Mom, David and his dad asked me to go fishing tomorrow!"

"Well, I'm sorry, but you'll have to do that another time."

"Mom! What if there isn't another time?"

"Look, we don't have time to discuss that now. The bottom line is this: We are all going to Grandma's, and we are all going to show her how much we love and appreciate her."

"Can't I just call her and tell her I love her? Why do I have to go?"

"Go pack! *Now!*"

○ Talk about It

- People talk about "making sacrifices" for those they love. Or they talk about how "costly" love is. What do those phrases mean?
- Talk about a time when someone went out of his or her way to demonstrate love for you.
- When have you made a sacrifice (or done without something) in order to show love to someone else?
- Do you think Scott is being selfish? Do you think his mom is being unreasonable?
- What are some sacrifices you could make this week to show love to a family member?

☑ Check It Out

When it comes to love, mere words are not enough—see John 13:34-35 and 1 John 3:18.

♡ Apply It

Love is more than feelings and sentiments; it is attitudes and actions. Jesus commanded us to love as he loved us (John 13:34-35). How? By helping when it's not convenient, by giving when it hurts, by devoting energy to others' welfare rather than our own, by absorbing hurts from others without complaining or fighting back. By sacrificing. This kind of loving is hard to do. That is why people notice when you do it and know you are empowered by God in the process. Make the choice to love as Jesus did.

▮▮ Tip for Parents

Keep your eyes open for teachable moments during your daily activities. A news story about a mom who maintains a bedside vigil with her comatose son or a magazine article about Mother Teresa or a radio request for donations to aid flood victims—everyday items like these are perfect opportunities to talk about the sacrificial aspect of love. Our children need to see that opportunities for showing sacrificial love are all around us all the time.

Safety

Tom, Wayne, and some other kids from the neighborhood are shooting baskets at the school playground when Benjamin comes riding up on his bike.

"Hey, guys! You gotta come see what I found! It's the best!"

Everybody looks at Benjamin with a mixture of suspicion and curiosity. (He has a reputation for exaggerating, but occasionally he *does* come up with a good idea.)

"What's up?" Wayne inquires.

"It's tunnels! All underneath the college. I heard my older brother talking about it, and so I followed him and his friends last night. Sure enough, they're there! All kinds of cool tunnels, big enough to walk in! C'mon, let's go check it out!"

The guys aren't sure whether to believe Benjamin.

Matthew is skeptical. "Are you trying to mess with us?"

"I'm serious! I saw 'em last night."

The guys hop on their bikes and pedal over to campus—trying not to act excited. Sure enough, Benjamin leads them behind the administration building, over near some Dumpsters, and shows them a steel grate that is loose. A ladder descends from ground level into the darkness.

"What do you say, guys? You wanna go for it?"

"Let's do it!" Michael shouts.

Tom is suddenly cautious. "Don't we need flashlights?"

Wayne nods. "He's right. We can't stumble around in the dark."

"OK," Matthew agrees, "let's all go home and get flashlights, candles, whatever you can find. We'll meet back here in half an hour."

The boys take off excitedly—all except Tom. He's thinking hard. What if somebody gets hurt? What if they get lost underground? He feels strongly that they shouldn't go down the ladder. But they'll never listen to him. *What should I do?* Tom wonders.

○ Talk about It

- Are you adventurous or not? Why?
- What is the craziest thing you have ever done?
- What options does Tom have?
- What would you do in Tom's situation?

☑ Check It Out

Read Proverbs 1:8-33.

♡ Apply It

Adventures can be fun. Many people, when called by God, have set off on adventures and done great things for him even when faced with danger (consider the Israelites who stormed Jericho, Daniel who went into the lions' den, Paul who braved beatings and imprisonments). However, not all danger is meant to be an invitation to adventure. Sometimes danger should be avoided, and the small voice of conscience and wisdom within should cause you to think twice. Going along with others in order to be a part of the crowd and engaging in a harmful or sinful activity is unwise, dangerous, and wrong. Believers must learn to make choices, not on the basis of short-range pleasure or the excitement of adventure, but in view of the long-range effects. This means steering clear of activities that we know are wrong.

♊ Tip for Parents

Children need to know the difference between keeping a confidence and keeping vital information secret. Try to explain to your kids the importance of sharing information about friends or siblings who might be in danger.

Salvation

At a slumber party, just after a pillow fight and just before a late-night snack, the conversation somehow or another took a sharp turn in an unexpected direction. Four girls, ages ten and eleven, found themselves talking about God, Jesus, Easter, heaven, hell, and eternity.

Their discussion went something like this:

"I know for sure I'm going to heaven."

"You do? For sure? How can you know that?"

"Because the Bible says so."

"Oh, really? Hmmm. I guess I never read that part. . . . But I'm pretty sure I'm going to heaven, too. I mean, I *do* believe in God and everything, and I for sure *don't* want to go to hell."

"So have you ever asked Jesus to be your Savior?"

"What do you mean?"

"She means all the stuff about Easter—you know, Jesus dying on the cross for our sins—and us putting our faith in him."

"Um, I don't know. What exactly is faith? How do I know if I have it?"

Just then, Mrs. Teague stuck her head in the door. "Does everybody want nachos?"

"Oh, Mom, I'm glad you're here. Tell Julie what faith is."

"What?"

○ Talk about It

- How would you explain faith to someone like Julie?
- Why does becoming a Christian involve more than just believing in God or knowing about what Jesus did?
- The Bible talks about salvation being a free gift. What does that mean?
- What are some of the blessings and benefits of salvation?
- How can a person know for sure whether he or she is a Christian?
- Do you know beyond a shadow of a doubt that you are going to spend eternity with God in heaven?

☑ Check It Out

To correctly understand this topic, check out these verses: John 3:16; Ephesians 2:8-9; and 1 John 5:11-13.

♡ Apply It

When some people learn that they are saved by God through faith, they start to worry. *Do I have enough faith?* they wonder. *Is my faith strong enough to save me?* If they're wondering about their sincerity, their questions have merit. But if they're wondering whether they have *enough* faith, or whether their faith is strong enough, their worry is not necessary. It is Jesus Christ who saves us, not our faith. All we need to do is have faith in him—any amount will do. He is strong enough to save us no matter how weak our faith, so long as it is genuine. Jesus offers us salvation as a gift because he loves us. The role of faith is to trust in Jesus Christ, to reach out and accept his wonderful gift of salvation.

♟ Tip for Parents

Pray regularly for the salvation of your children. Pray that they will not merely "borrow" your faith or "parrot" your beliefs but that they will meet Christ in a genuine, life-changing way. Nothing in the world is more critical than that our children understand and embrace the truth of the gospel.

Satan

Trick-or-treaters had been coming to the Stinsons' door for about an hour when two little boys showed up dressed as devils.

After she dropped some candy into their jack-o'-lanterns, Mrs. Stinson turned to her son Mitch and said, "I don't like that."

"What?"

"Parents letting their kids dress up like the devil."

"How come?"

"Because it's not funny or cute."

"What do you mean?"

"I mean that Satan is real, and I don't think we should make him out to be a harmless little creature with a pitchfork."

"Does he have a pitchfork?"

"I don't think so. At least, I've never read in the Bible about him having one."

"So what *does* the devil look like, Mom?"

"I'm not sure. I think before he fell to earth, he was the most beautiful of all the angels."

"What? You mean the devil used to be an *angel?*"

"Yeah. He and all the demons are fallen angels."

"I never knew that."

"I think he'd prefer that you never did. He's a liar and the father of lies. Better pay attention in Sunday school!"

⟳ Talk about It

- Why is there so much interest in Satan and the occult in our country?
- C. S. Lewis said that most people make one of two mistakes when it comes to the devil: They either deny that he exists, or they see demons behind every bush. What do you think of that statement?
- What do you know about the devil?
- Can the devil make us do wrong things? How do you know?
- What are demons, and what do they do?
- Why don't Christians have to fear the devil?

☑ Check It Out

Find out about Satan's origins, activities, and future in Isaiah 14:12-14; 1 Peter 5:8; and Revelation 20:7-10.

♡ Apply It

Disguised as a crafty serpent, Satan came to tempt Eve (Genesis 3:1). Satan at one time was an angel who rebelled against God and was thrown out of heaven. As a created being, Satan has definite limitations. Although he is trying to tempt everyone to turn away from God, he will not be the final victor. In Genesis 3:14-15, God promises that Satan will be crushed by one of the woman's offspring, the Messiah, Jesus Christ.

▐▌ Tip for Parents

Don't allow anything occult-related to enter your house. Tarot cards, crystals, Ouija boards—those items together with activities like astrology, palm reading, and séances can give the devil a foothold in your life or in the life of your family. Like the angel Michael in Jude 1:9, we need to *respect* the devil's power. But because of the power of the Lord Jesus Christ, we do not have to *fear* Satan (1 John 4:4).

Secrets

On a hot day, Robert and Jeremie ride their bikes down to the neighborhood convenience store to get a soft drink.

After paying for his strawberry drink, Robert is standing by the door looking at a motorcycle parked out front. Suddenly, out of the corner of his eye, he notices Jeremie casually take a candy bar off the shelf and slide it into his pants' pocket.

Robert almost chokes on a swallow of drink! He can't believe he just witnessed his older brother stealing something! from a store!

As they're riding their bikes back home, Robert's heart is pounding. He keeps waiting for Jeremie to say something. But he never does. Obviously he doesn't realize that Robert *saw* him shoplift the candy bar.

All the rest of that evening, Robert wonders what to do. Should he say something to Jeremie? Should he tell his parents? Should he just forget it? Later he starts worrying about what might happen if the *police* show up at their house. And what if they find out that Robert *saw* Jeremie steal the candy bar and that he didn't say or do anything about it? He might get in trouble, too!

○ Talk about It

- Why do you think people shoplift?
- How would you feel about shoplifting if you were a store owner?
- When is it right to keep secrets? When is it wrong?
- What would you do in Robert's situation?
- What are the consequences if Robert does nothing? if Robert confronts Jeremie? if Robert tells his parents?

☑ Check It Out

Read James 5:19-20 and apply it to the situation you just read about.

♡ Apply It

The apostle Paul did not enjoy reprimanding his friends and fellow believers, but he cared enough about them to confront them with their wrongdoing (2 Corinthians 2:4). Proverbs 27:6 says, "Wounds from a friend are better than many kisses from an enemy." Sometimes our friends make choices that we know are wrong. If we ignore their behavior and let them continue in it, we aren't showing love to them. We show love by honestly sharing our concerns in order to help those friends do and be their very best for God. When we don't make any move to help, we show that we are more concerned about being well liked than about what will happen to them.

♟ Tip for Parents

It might be wise to list for your children some situations in which you don't want your kids keeping secrets (e.g., drug use by a friend, sexual abuse, talk of suicide by anyone). The more situations you spell out overtly, the less chance there is of an avoidable tragedy. Perhaps you and your children can hammer out a good rule of thumb for determining when secrets are good and acceptable.

Self-Control

Annie gets home from work and immediately opens the refrigerator. There sits what's left of a delicious cheesecake. She hesitates. Her conscience is saying, *Don't do it! You're on a diet, remember?* But her stomach is growling and saying, *Aw, c'mon! You had a rough day. You deserve a little pleasure here. And, besides, who's gonna be hurt?*

Moments later Annie plops down on the couch with her hefty hunk of dessert. She looks at the huge folder on the coffee table. There are enough tests and assignments in that folder to wallpaper her whole garage. She's really behind in her grading, and she knows she needs to get right after it. *I'll do it later,* she thinks as she reaches for the remote control.

In about an hour, Annie's son Tim gets home from mowing the neighbor's yard. He's covered with wet grass, and as he tromps across the living-room carpet, he leaves a trail behind him.

Annie can't stand it. She starts yelling, "Tim, how many times have I told you to wipe your feet?"

◯ Talk about It

- What kinds of situations cause you to lose control? Why?
- How would you define *self-control*? What does the Bible mean when it uses that term?
- Why do certain situations get to us more than others?
- Why do some things bother you that might not bother someone else?
- What is the difference between self-control and being controlled by the Spirit?
- What are some areas of your life where you need to begin exercising self-control?

☑ Check It Out

Consider these verses that advocate self-control: Proverbs 25:28 and Galatians 5:16-25.

♡ Apply It

In the days of the early church, some false teachers said that self-control was not important because deeds do not save us from sin (2 Peter 2:19). It is true that deeds cannot save us, but it is false to think they do not matter. We are saved so we can grow to resemble Christ and become servants of others. God wants to produce his character in us, but this requires our discipline and effort. As we obey Christ, who guides us by his Spirit, we will develop greater and greater self-control over our appetites and emotions (2 Peter 1:6).

♟ Tip for Parents

Biblical self-control is impossible—if we try to accomplish or achieve it in our own strength. We can't rein in our tongues, appetites, tempers, or thoughts. They are far too unruly. But the Spirit of God *can* enable us to say no to unhealthy urges or unwise notions. Quit trusting in your own strength, and start relying on the power of the Holy Spirit. This is the only way to be what God wants you to be.

Service

At church on Sunday, one of the deacons made an announcement at the end of the service about the upcoming workday. A workday is a twice-a-year service project in which the members of the church gather to spruce up the church facilities. Everyone gathers early on a Saturday to sweep, mop, scrub, paint, change lightbulbs, organize—in short, to do *whatever* needs to be done. It's always a tiring day, but it gives everyone a sense of ownership and involvement and pride. And what's more, everyone celebrates at the end of the day with a giant barbecue, complete with volleyball, games, and more.

On the way home from church, the Smith children were talking about workday. "I signed up to help in the youth room!" Justin announced before asking his older brother Cliff, "What about you?"

Cliff mumbled, *"I'm* not going. I've already got plans. Besides, why would I want to give up a whole Saturday to go do a bunch of stuff the church janitor ought to be doing anyway?"

"Cliff!" exclaimed Mrs. Smith. "I can't believe your attitude! You need to help pitch in. What makes you think you're exempt from serving?"

Cliff shrugged. "Well, Dad's not going, so why should I?"

Mrs. Smith turned and gave her husband a surprised, hurt look. *"You're* not going? Since when?"

"Hey, I'd *love* to help out, but who has time? If I do *anything* this weekend, I need to be doing odd jobs around *our* house!"

↻ Talk about It

- What are some ways people help out at your church?
- Why are so many Christians reluctant to sign up for service opportunities?
- What would happen if every church member adopted the attitude of Cliff and his dad?
- Talk about a time when you were involved in some kind of service and you really had fun. Why do you think it was so enjoyable?
- How does it feel to serve people who only want to be served?
- What are some specific ways you could serve today?

☑ Check It Out

See the importance of serving in Galatians 5:13 and 1 Peter 4:10-11.

♡ Apply It

Jesus was a model servant (John 13:1-17). Washing guests' feet was a job for a household servant to carry out when guests arrived. But Jesus wrapped a towel around his waist, as any slave would do, and washed and dried his disciples' feet. If even he, God in the flesh, is willing to serve, we his followers should also be servants, willing to help in any way that glorifies God. Be willing to follow Christ's example of serving. Think of someone you can serve today. God gives a blessing to those who agree that humble service is Christ's way and also follow through (13:17).

♟ Tip for Parents

Servanthood has always been an endangered character quality. "What's in it for me?" is the all-natural attitude of raw human nature. Our kids will never learn to serve unless we teach them *why* that is significant, *what* that means, and *how* to live such a lifestyle. Consider implementing a regular, ongoing, family service project. Taking time out to expend the effort (and sometimes money) to help others communicates volumes about the imperative nature of service.

Sin

Uncle Gregg and his wife, Stacey, came to church with the Mouton family this weekend, and the kids were eager to know what he thought. (Only twenty-five years old, he's their favorite uncle, even if he's not "into" spiritual things.)

"So, Uncle Gregg, how'd you like church?"

"It was all right. I really liked the music."

"What about the sermon?"

"What about it?"

"Did you agree with it?"

"Not totally. I just don't see why preachers harp so much on *sin*. I haven't been to church in five years. And the first time I go back, I basically get told that I'm a sinner."

"Well, you are. We all are."

"Says who?"

"God—in the Bible. Weren't you listening?"

"Look, I make mistakes. We all do. But I'm basically a good person. You guys know that. I've never done anything really bad, and I have no desire to. So you're going to sit there and say that I'm a bad person and that I'm 'separated from God'? C'mon!"

The kids look at their dad. They don't know what to say.

♻ Talk about It

- What is sin? How would you define it?
- Why does sin matter so much to God?
- What if a person really does live a good, moral life? Is he or she still a sinner?
- What would you say to someone like Uncle Gregg?
- What are the consequences of sin? (Hint: See Romans 6:23.) What about the remedy for sin?
- Do you know for sure that your sins have been forgiven?

☑ Check It Out

Read Romans 3:9-12, 23 for a clear statement of the sinfulness of each person.

♡ Apply It

All people are unacceptable to God in their sinful condition (Romans 3:10-18). It is only the blood of Christ that makes us clean in God's sight. Have you recognized your need for Christ, or do you say to yourself, *I'm not too bad. I'm a pretty good person*? Look at these verses and see if any of them apply to you. Have you ever lied? Have you ever hurt someone's feelings by your words or tone of voice? Are you ever bitter toward anyone? Do you become angry with those who strongly disagree with you? In thought, word, and deed you, like everyone else in the world, stand guilty before God. We must remember who we are in his sight—alienated sinners. Don't deny that you are a sinner. Instead, allow your desperate need to point you toward Christ.

♟ Tip for Parents

Do not assume that your children will somehow "pick up the gospel." They need to have it explained to them. And that is a process that works best over time. Few people can grasp the magnitude of what Christ has done for us in one short conversation. The idea (and reality) of sin must be grappled with and grasped. The sobering fact of death (i.e., spiritual separation from God) must be understood. The work of Christ needs to be explained carefully and accurately. Finally, the concepts of grace and faith need to be clearly conveyed.

Consult your pastor or local Christian bookstore for the names of some good, age-appropriate tools for helping your children understand the love of Christ.

Skipping School

Raymond attends a big, public junior high school. One of his friends is Garrett. Garrett lives right across the street from school, and his mom works full-time. No one is at Garrett's house during the day. So about twice a month, Garrett and Raymond casually slip away from school just before the opening bell rings and cross the street. There at Garrett's they watch TV, hang out, and just enjoy not being in class.

Altogether the boys have skipped seven days of school this year. And so far no one has even noticed. Their school-skipping plan is working perfectly.

⟳ Talk about It

- What do you think about what Raymond and Garrett are doing?
- What are the chances that the boys will get caught?
- Obviously, the idea of no school is fun to think about, but what are some of the negative consequences for people who don't attend classes?
- What would you say to Raymond or Garrett if they were your friends? if they asked you to join them?
- (For parents) What would you do if you found out your children were skipping school?

☑ Check It Out

In addition to being foolish and lazy, those who skip school are being dishonest. See what God says about dishonesty in Proverbs 12:13, 17, 19, and 22.

♡ Apply It

Living right is like posting a guard for your life (Proverbs 13:6). Every choice for good sets into motion other opportunities for good. Evil choices follow the same pattern to the opposite effect. Every choice, in other words, paves the way for the next one. Each decision you make to obey God's Word brings a greater sense of order to your life, while each decision to disobey will bring confusion and destruction. The right choices you make stand you in good stead and protect you from the consequences of poor choices. Obedience brings the greatest safety and security.

♦♦ Tip for Parents

It is important to distinguish between occasional childhood lapses of judgment and habitual wrong behavior. Children are naturally curious and, in the course of their growing up, often commit foolish, but largely "innocent," acts (e.g., accepting a dare to jump out of a tree, pelting passing cars with snowballs or water balloons, or the old standard, hitting a baseball through a neighbor's window). Wise parents recognize these common occurrences and take them in stride. They use them to teach truth; they do not blow them out of proportion. By making a huge deal out of normal childhood experiences, some parents end up exacerbating the problem.

Standing Up for Rights

Walking out of the courthouse, the Quigleys are furious.

Four months ago, they paid $850 to the Harrison Flooring Company for the installation of a new, vinyl kitchen floor. The balance of $850 was to be paid upon the satisfactory completion of the job.

But almost immediately things began to get fishy. The store manager claimed he had the flooring in stock but couldn't find an installer. Then he wouldn't return phone calls. Then the building was locked up tight during normal business hours. At last the truth came out—the owners were filing for bankruptcy protection.

The Quigleys tried every avenue to get their money back. They met with Mr. Harrison, his attorney, and a representative for the bank and were promised a refund. It never came. They contacted the district attorney's office and the Better Business Bureau. That got them nowhere. They finally tried to work out a deal with Harrison's landlord—to let them into the padlocked building so they could at least get the flooring they had paid for. That proved to be another dead end.

Just a few minutes ago, a bankruptcy judge essentially told the Quigleys, "Sorry. There's nothing you can do. Be glad you didn't lose more."

"That is so unfair!" Cindi yelled as the Quigleys climbed into their minivan. "They rip us off, and then they are protected by the law. Where's the protection for innocent consumers like us?"

"If I weren't a Christian," her husband snapped, "I'd go punch Mark Harrison in the nose!"

○ Talk about It

- Have you ever been scammed or ripped off? How?
- Do you feel that any of your rights are being trampled these days? Which ones?
- What do you think of the true story above?
- How does it feel to be taken advantage of?
- Christ commanded us to turn the other cheek (Matthew 5:39). In what way does this apply to situations like the one the Quigleys encountered? In what way does it not apply?
- In what situations is it appropriate for Christians to "grin and bear it" or "silently suffer"?

☑ Check It Out

There were times in Paul's life when he let people mistreat and take advantage of him, but there were also times when he insisted on his rights under the law—see Acts 22:25 and Acts 25:10-11.

♡ Apply It

Jesus told us not to retaliate (Matthew 5:43-44), in part to keep us from taking the law into our own hands. The punishment of evildoers is the job of government (Romans 13:4); reforming them is ours. By loving and praying for our enemies, we overcome evil with good.

Some religious leaders interpreted Leviticus 19:18 as teaching that they should love only those who loved in return, and Psalms 139:19-22 and 140:9-11 as meaning that they should hate their enemies. But Jesus said that we should love our enemies. If you love your enemies and treat them well, you will truly show that Jesus is Lord of your life. That is possible only for those who give themselves fully to God, because only he can deliver people from natural selfishness. Trust the Holy Spirit to help you show love to those for whom you have no feelings of love.

Tip for Parents

We need to help our children develop the quality of meekness. The biblical quality of meekness—also translated *gentleness*—conveys the idea of strength under control. Moses and Jesus each possessed this rare quality. They were normally gentle and kind, but in sinful or unjust circumstances, they displayed great power.

Stealing

Last week when Rob and his friends walked over to a nearby convenience store to get a snack, Rob watched in envy as his buddies purchased soft drinks, candy bars, and bags of chips. Rob couldn't buy anything—he had no money, not even any change.

But while he was standing there watching his friends enjoy all their goodies, he thought of his dad's big jar of change at home. Actually, it's a big glass water jug—like the kind you see on a water cooler at an office building.

The jug is more than half full, and Rob figures it must weigh over a hundred pounds. There's no telling how much money is in it.

Suddenly Rob is thinking about all the snacks he could buy with all that money. He's realizing that his dad probably wouldn't miss a handful of that change every now and then. He's trying to figure when the best time would be to slip into his dad's closet and sneak out a few quarters.

Immediately something inside Rob protests: *You can't take your dad's change—that's stealing.* But just as quickly another voice inside him rationalizes: *Yeah, but think about all the jobs you do around the house for which you don't get paid. Besides, that money is just sitting in the closet. Your dad isn't even using it. There's nothing wrong with enjoying a snack with a few friends. And it's not like you're going to do it every day.*

Rob tells his friends he'll see them later, and he runs down the street toward his house.

○ Talk about It

- Why are we sometimes tempted to take things that don't belong to us?
- How do you feel when someone steals something of yours?
- What does it mean to "rationalize" or "justify" your wrong actions?
- What are some of the consequences of stealing?

☑ Check It Out

Read Exodus 20:15 and Leviticus 19:11.

♡ Apply It

While it is obvious from the Ten Commandments that God says not to steal, sometimes it's easy to rationalize. We can figure out a way for an action to not really be stealing. Besides, we can justify our actions by glibly saying, "It doesn't matter," "Everybody's doing it," or "Nobody will ever know." Do you find yourself making excuses for sin? Rationalizing sin makes it easier to commit, but rationalization does not convince God it's OK or cancel the punishment.

♊ Tip for Parents

The most powerful sermon against stealing is a life committed to honesty and integrity. If your kids see you obeying copyright laws (by not illegally copying music or videos), paying your fair share of income taxes, and giving back the extra change the store clerk accidentally gave you, they will be more likely to think twice themselves before yielding to the temptation to steal.

Stress

A minute ago, Ellen Bedford was in the kitchen banging pots and pans and yelling about pretty much everything.

Suddenly, she burst into tears and ran to her bedroom.

The men of the Bedford house, Lance, and sons, Kyle, nine, and Sean, seven, sit in silence around the breakfast table, wide-eyed, each wondering, *What in the world has gotten into her?*

Finally, Mr. Bedford speaks. "All right, guys, here's the deal. Mom's really stressed out. This new job as a real estate agent is taking its toll on her. And I don't think we've been too helpful here at home. We need to take some of the load off of her. So let's clean up the dishes here. Then I'll take you guys to school. And if I can get off early, I'll pick you up from basketball practice, OK? Oh, and how about we tell Mom *we'll* cook dinner tonight?"

"Us cook? Dad, are you crazy?"

"OK, how 'bout we tell Mom we'll stop and get pizza?"

"That's a better plan."

⟳ Talk about It

- What is stress? What causes it?
- How do you tend to react to stressful situations?
- How can a person tell when he or she is trying to do too much?
- Who in your family faces the most stress? How do you know?
- What specifically could you do to take the load off of someone who is wilting under the pressure of too much responsibility?

☑ Check It Out

Look at what happened when Jethro realized his son-in-law Moses was ›
stressed out from taking on too many responsibilities—Exodus 18:17-18,
22-23.

♡ Apply It

Moses once had a stress-induced crisis. He was spending so much time
and energy hearing the Hebrews' complaints that he could not get to
other important work. His father-in-law, Jethro, suggested that he delegate
most of this work to others and focus his efforts on jobs only he could do
(Exodus 18:13-26). People in positions of responsibility sometimes feel
that they are the only ones who can do necessary tasks, but others are
capable of handling part of the load. Delegation relieved Moses' stress
and improved the quality of the government. It helped prepare the people
for the system of government set up in Canaan. Distribute the load so no
one gets overloaded.

♟♟ Tip for Parents

Even organized families get stressed out. But disorganization is a surefire
way to put yourself over the edge! Institute a weekly family meeting at
which everyone catches up, compares schedules, and reminds each other
of upcoming events. This can be a good forum for giving out job assignments and/or asking for help. It can also be a good evaluation time. Perhaps some needless activities can be eliminated from the family calendar.

Studies

Fourteen-year-old Kelly is in constant demand as a baby-sitter. No wonder. She's great with kids—gentle, fun, patient, and extremely responsible. Whenever a big social event comes up, some of the younger couples at church jokingly "fight" over Kelly.

Last month one couple, the Moores, called Kelly a lot. In one sense she was glad—the Moores pay extremely well. But the downside of this "baby-sitting bonanza" was that Kelly was out late on a number of school nights. Since the Moores have two active boys under the age of five, Kelly was never able to study until around nine, and by then she was too exhausted to concentrate.

In short, over a three-week span, Kelly failed to complete a number of homework assignments, and she did poorly on several tests.

Today when report cards came out, Kelly's grades were lower than normal. Now her parents are telling her that she can no longer baby-sit on school nights.

"But, Mom, look at how much money I made!"

"I don't care about that. I care about your grades!"

"I still made straight B's!"

"Yes, but last term you made three A's."

"I'll study harder this time."

"I'm glad to hear that, but you're still not baby-sitting on school nights. Your studies have to come first."

⟳ Talk about It

- In the story above, who is right and who is wrong? Why do you feel this way?
- In addition to working, what other activities can cause a person's schoolwork to suffer?
- How (if at all) can students be involved in work or other extracurricular activities and still do well in school?

☑ Check It Out

Note that Solomon valued wisdom more than money or anything else— 1 Kings 3:7-13.

♡ Apply It

When given a chance to have anything in the world, Solomon asked for wisdom—"a discerning heart"—in order to lead well and to make right decisions. Solomon asked for wisdom ("discernment"), not wealth, but God gave him riches and long life as well. While God does not promise riches to those who follow him, he gives us what we need if we put his kingdom, his interests, and his principles first (Matthew 6:31-33). Setting your sights on riches will only leave you dissatisfied, because even if you get the riches you crave, you will still want something more. But if you put God and his work first, he will satisfy your deepest needs.

♟ Tip for Parents

Consider having a family goal-setting time to talk about priorities. Let each person set some realistic goals, and make some for the whole family as well. Then pray for each other, and hold each other accountable. Having clearly defined goals can keep us from jumbled priorities.

Success

They probably wouldn't admit it to just anyone, but deep down inside, each of the following individuals feels like a failure. See if you can relate to any of them.

Mrs. Kirk looks at her crazy, hectic life as a stay-at-home mom. She feels she spends most of her waking hours either in the laundry room, at the stove, or behind the wheel of her car. With three young kids, she envies her friends who have school-age children and who are able to work and use their college degrees.

At the men's retreat last weekend Mark Wagner ended up in a discussion group with a doctor, two lawyers, and another man who owns his own insurance business. The other guys were friendly, yet Mark felt out of place. As he told his wife later, "I just work for the city. Those guys probably thought I was a real loser."

Courtney Brown has a popular older brother who is an honor roll student and who sings solos in church all the time. Everyone is always raving about Tyler. "I hate following in his footsteps!" Courtney moans. "He's so perfect, and I'm so average!"

Jeffrey Lee is one of the only guys at Trenton Academy who doesn't play sports. No one has ever said anything to him, but since athletics are such a major deal in Trenton, Jeffrey is sure people think he is a sissy.

⟳ Talk about It

- What measuring stick(s) does our society use to determine who is successful and who is not?
- How would you define success?
- Who is the most successful person you know? Why do you say this?
- What would you say to each of the individuals above if they admitted to you their feelings of failure?
- In what areas do you feel unsuccessful? Why?

☑ Check It Out

Read God's definition of success in Joshua 1:6-9.

♡ Apply It

Many people think that prosperity and success come from having power, influential personal contacts, and a relentless desire to get ahead. But the strategy for gaining prosperity that God taught Joshua goes against such criteria. He said that to succeed, Joshua must (1) be strong and courageous, (2) obey God's law, and (3) constantly read and study the Book of the Law—God's Word. If you want to be successful, follow God's instructions to Joshua. You may not succeed by the world's standards, but you will be a success in God's eyes—and his opinion lasts forever.

▮▮ Tip for Parents

Try to praise your kids less for things like looks and accomplishments, and more for things like demonstrations of Christian character and maturity.

Suffering

Why do some people have to go through so much grief?

About four years ago, Amanda lost both her parents in an automobile accident.

Despite the shock and pain, she and her siblings managed to pull together and carry on.

Then about a year ago, Amanda's sister was killed in another wreck.

Says one friend, "It's just so crazy. You wonder, *Why, God? Why so much tragedy for one family?* And then you think, *Why is* my *life so blessed and free of that kind of suffering?* It's kind of scary, because you know bad things happen in this world—even to people who love God. So sometimes I catch myself waiting for something terrible to happen.

"I don't know what I'd do in that situation. Would I hate God? or stop believing in him? It's hard to say. But I do know this: Amanda's trust is amazing. She's such an example to so many people. I have so much admiration for her."

⟳ Talk about It

- What is the most painful thing you've ever had to face?
- Why is there so much suffering in this world?
- If God is good, and if he's all-powerful, why does he let bad things happen to people?
- Is there any good that can come out of suffering? What?
- What could your family do today to encourage someone like Amanda?

☑ Check It Out

Read about the certainty of suffering (Job 5:7 and John 16:33) as well as the value of suffering (Romans 5:3-4; 8:18).

♡ Apply It

We suffer for many reasons. Some suffering is the direct result of our own sin; some happens because of our foolishness; some results from simply living in a fallen world. Peter wrote about suffering that comes as a result of doing good (1 Peter 2:21-23). Christ never sinned, and yet he suffered so that we could be set free. When we follow Christ's example and live for others, we too may suffer. Our goal should be to face suffering as he did—with patience, calmness, and confidence that God is in control of our life.

▌▐ Tip for Parents

Teach your children how to comfort those who are hurting. Help them to see that the best response is usually just to be with those in pain and listen to them. Discourage them from being like Job's "comforters"—offering theological reasons and sermons and lectures. Suffering folks rarely need (or want) books or Bible verses; they do not want glib platitudes or empty-sounding promises. Instead, they need lots of hugs and love.

Teasing

There's a new kid at school. Trevor Tuggle is his name, and the other kids have been giving him a hard time.

They tease him because he talks funny. They laugh at him on the playground because he's terrible at kickball. They make fun of him in the hallway because he usually has some message taped to the back of his shirt that says "Ignore me!" or "I can't help it if I'm stupid."

Today Jenny and Lisa came home really upset.

"What's wrong?" their mother quizzed them.

"Well, it has to do with Trevor."

"Who's Trevor?"

"The new kid at school."

"What about him?"

"Well, everybody teases him. Sometimes *we've* even made fun of him. Anyway, today at recess some of the guys were playing tackle the man with the ball. And all of a sudden somebody grabbed Trevor and tackled him."

"So why is that bad? I would think as the new kid he would *want* to be included."

"No, Mom. Remember? It was picture day today, and he was wearing his good coat and tie! And, anyway, they just stuffed the football inside his jacket, and then they all tackled him in the mud. And when they got off him he just sat there in the mud crying. He's never even gotten upset before. And everybody else was laughing at him. But Jenny and I felt awful!"

Tears were rolling down Lisa's nodding face. "I'm never gonna tease anybody again!"

Talk about It

- Why do some people just naturally seem to get picked on?
- How does it feel to be made fun of?
- What determines whether a person is special or valuable? Why?
- If you were Jenny or Lisa, what would you do the next time you went to school?
- Who is someone that you can stick up for (rather than make fun of) today?
- What does it mean to say that we are created in the image of God?

☑ Check It Out

It's easy to forget that every person is special and loved by God. There are no exceptions. Read Genesis 1:26-27 and Psalm 139.

♡ Apply It

In God's eyes, a person's value has no relationship to his or her wealth or position on the social ladder. Many people who have excelled in God's work began in poverty or humble beginnings. God supersedes the social orders of this world, often choosing his future leaders and ambassadors from among social outcasts (Psalm 113:5-9). Many of his most notable servants, such as Moses, David, Daniel, and Paul, had no aspirations for greatness. Do you treat the unwanted in society as though they have value? Demonstrate by your actions that all people are valuable and useful in God's eyes.

Tip for Parents

The *Jesus* film (produced and distributed by Campus Crusade for Christ) accurately portrays the life of Christ from his birth to his resurrection. It demonstrates vividly how kindly and gently he treated those who were different and/or who were social outcasts. Watch this movie with your family and discuss it.

Television

The Sandersons don't watch much television, but one program they have always enjoyed viewing together is *Gone to the Dogs*. The show is a sitcom about the Thompson family, a young couple with twin teenagers who inherit a thriving pet store from a long-lost uncle.

When the show first came out, it was uproariously funny. The scripts were really witty and well written, and the acting was top-notch. The humor was relatively clean, and there was nothing objectionable at all about the characters or the situations presented.

The last few episodes, however, have featured a wisecracking new employee (a college student who is interested in the Thompsons' daughter). Suddenly the dialogue has become slightly suggestive, and the jokes have become a bit off-color.

Mrs. Sanderson is of the opinion that the family should stop watching *Gone to the Dogs*. Mr. Sanderson isn't so sure. "It's still one of the cleanest programs on TV. Besides, it's the top-rated show."

The Sanderson kids don't see what the big fuss is all about. All their friends at school watch *Gone to the Dogs* and talk about it all the time. They want to keep watching.

◯ Talk about It

- What is your favorite television program? Why?
- What features of your favorite TV show are positive and what elements are not?
- Some Christians get rid of their TVs altogether; others try to view selectively. Which approach do you think is best and why?
- What standards should we use to decide whether or not to watch a particular television program?

☑ Check It Out

How does Philippians 4:8 relate to this particular discussion?

♡ Apply It

What we put into our minds determines what comes out in our words and actions. In Philippians 4:8, Paul tells us to program our minds with thoughts that are true, noble, right, pure, lovely, admirable, excellent, and praiseworthy. Examine what you are putting into your mind through television, books, conversations, movies, and magazines. Replace harmful input with wholesome material. Above all, read God's Word and pray. Ask God to help you focus your mind on what is good and pure. It takes practice, but it can be done.

♟ Tip for Parents

Here's an idea for gaining control of the TV habit in your home. Allow each family member a certain number of hours of TV viewing per week (you set the standards). Family members are then billed for the privilege of watching additional programs. Use this "penalty money" for a good cause. You can set up a related program of paying children a small amount for each book read.

Temptation

On Friday afternoon, the four members of the Wallace family each faced a serious temptation.

Peter, forty-one, got a fourth phone call from a persistent young man who had been sending in manuscripts for possible publication. "Hey, Mr. Wallace, this is Cary McNeal. Sorry to bother you again. I'm just wondering if you have had a chance to look at the materials I sent you?" Peter immediately felt twinges of guilt for not having returned the man's calls. *Should I tell him the truth?* Peter wondered. There was a long awkward silence, then Peter . . .

Bonnie (age a big secret) walked out of the grocery store and suddenly realized that the clerk had given her change for a twenty-dollar bill instead of a ten. She paused, remembered the long lines at the checkout, looked at her watch, thought about rush-hour traffic, and . . .

Meredith, sixteen, entered her English-literature class only to hear the teacher announce a pop quiz. Midway through the test, Meredith felt a nudge in her back. It was Keith, the class genius, offering her the correct answers on a scrap of paper. Meredith looked both ways, thought for a long moment, and . . .

Matthew, thirteen, saw a crowd of guys clustered around a locker. "Hey, Sean, what's up?" they inquired. Sean smiled and said, "Aw, man, Wheeler has a *Penthouse!* Come see!" Matthew froze in his tracks, gulped, and . . .

○ Talk about It

- What choices do you think the people above made?
- Is it a sin to be tempted? Why do you say that?
- Why are temptations different for different people?
- Talk about a time when you yielded to temptation and when you resisted temptation.
- What is your best strategy for saying no to sinful impulses?

☑ Check It Out

For a reminder of how God can strengthen us to withstand temptation, read Hebrews 2:18; James 4:7; and 1 Corinthians 10:13.

♡ Apply It

A person has not shown true obedience if he or she has never had an opportunity to disobey. We read in Deuteronomy 8:2 that God led Israel into the desert to humble and test them. God wanted his people to see whether they would obey him when it came time to choose. You, too, will be tested every day. Because you know that testing will come, be alert and ready for it. Remember, pressure situations don't break your convictions, they reveal them. Hold on to your Christian ways under pressure . . . when it counts most.

♛♛ Tip for Parents

It might be wise to have your family memorize one of the verses just cited. Make it a project, even a contest, and then say it together on occasion. You never know how this might help a family member in a tough situation.

Tithing

What do you think you'd discover if you could read people's minds when the offering plate is passed at church?

Here's what each of the Bagwells was thinking on Sunday:

- Mr. Bagwell dropped a check into the plate and thought, *Boy, I hope next week when they announce the bid results, God remembers that I gave this money.*
- Mrs. Bagwell watched their hard-earned money go into the plate and prayed silently: *God, thanks for blessing us like you have. Please use this gift to reach more people with the gospel.*
- Marty Bagwell reluctantly contributed fifty cents out of his five-dollar allowance and thought, *Why does Mom make me do this? I need this more than the church does!*
- Little Chelsea waited until the plate was right in front of her, *then* she got out her coin purse and dropped in a handful of pennies. Looking around, she noticed several people staring at her. She smiled and then suddenly felt embarrassed.

⟳ Talk about It

- Which of the Bagwells had good attitudes? bad attitudes? Why?
- If God doesn't need our money, why should we give?
- What is tithing, and how is it like/unlike giving?
- How do you honestly feel when you give or tithe? Why?
- Some people say, "One tenth belongs to God, and the rest is yours." Do you agree with that statement? Why or why not?
- Studies show that the average church member or family only gives about 3 percent of its income. What do you think about that?

☑ Check It Out

Read two passages about giving—2 Corinthians 9:6-9 and Luke 21:1-4.

♡ Apply It

How do you decide how much to give? The Bible gives us several principles to follow (2 Corinthians 8:1–9:15): (1) Each person should follow through on previous promises (8:10-11; 9:3); (2) each person should give as much as he or she is able (8:12; 9:6); (3) each person must make up his or her own mind how much to give (9:7); and (4) each person should give in proportion to what God has given him or her (9:10). God gives to us so that we can give to others.

The attitude with which we give is more important than the amount we give. We don't have to be embarrassed if we can give only a small gift. God is concerned about *how* we give from the resources we have (Mark 12:41-44).

♊ Tip for Parents

As a rule, kids whose parents encourage and teach them how to give grow up likely to continue that habit. Make sure your kids understand the principle that everything we have belongs to God (Psalm 24:1).

Tobacco

Nine-year-old Cedrick practically drags his friend Rod behind the corner of the building. "C'mon," he encourages. "I've got something to show you."

When they get completely hidden away in the back drive, Cedrick digs deeply in his coat pocket and produces a mangled pack of cigarettes.

"Where'd you get those?"

"Some guy who came to see my sister. I took them out of his car."

"You gonna smoke one?"

"Well, I didn't bring them back here to look at them."

Cedrick retrieves the box of matches from his other pocket, and the boys light up. Rod's first puff is followed by a fit of coughing.

Cedrick just laughs. "Man, you don't know what you're doing! Haven't you ever smoked before?"

"Sure I have. All the time. I just never tried this brand. It's different. It has a stronger taste."

The boys practice holding the cigarettes in different ways. They try blowing smoke through their noses. They attempt to blow smoke rings.

In about twenty minutes, Rod feels like he's going to throw up. "I gotta go home and use the bathroom," he announces.

"So how'd you like 'em?"

"Great," Rod responds weakly. "Those are really good."

○ Talk about It

- Should Christians smoke? Why or why not?
- What are the drawbacks to smoking?
- Why do you think people smoke?

☑ Check It Out

Read 1 Corinthians 6:19-20. Even though the context of this passage is avoiding sexual immorality, how does the principle apply to the use of tobacco?

♡ Apply It

Many people say they have the right to do whatever they want with their own bodies. Although they think that this is freedom, they are really enslaved to their own desires. When we become Christians, the Holy Spirit fills and lives in us. Therefore, we no longer own our bodies. Christ's death freed us from sin but also obligated us to his service. If you live in a building owned by someone else, you try not to violate the building's rules. Because your body belongs to God, you must not violate his standards for living.

▮▮ Tip for Parents

Most kids will steer clear of the tobacco habit if, when they are young, a strong, concerted effort is made to show them all the negatives of smoking. One father took his young children (ages five to eight) into a smoke-filled restaurant for a meal and used that unpleasant experience as a wonderful teaching moment.

The Tongue

The Arabies love their new cordless telephone. They can walk around the house—even out into the yard—talking to friends and still keep an eye on the children.

There's nothing all that unusual about the Arabies' phone habits. Kelly chats with her best friend, Stacy, almost daily. They discuss life and events and people in the small town of Jonesboro. Trey, on the other hand, hates the phone. You'll rarely catch him "reaching out and touching someone." However, he does have a couple of college buddies who call pretty regularly. One friend, Brad, calls to tell Trey jokes— many of them off-color, a few downright dirty. Trey listens politely, and sometimes he truly laughs at his old fraternity brother's jokes.

This afternoon, Kelly was sitting on the front porch talking on the phone to Stacy when the little girl from next door came riding up the driveway. "Mrs. Kelly," she said, "did you know that sometimes when my mom tries to use our phone, she can hear you and Mr. Trey talking on your cordless phone?"

Kelly almost fell out of her rocking chair. "Stacy," she blurts, "let me go inside and call you back on the other phone."

☿ Talk about It

- What do you like and dislike about talking on the phone?
- Why was Kelly so shocked to discover that her neighbors could overhear her phone conversations?
- How do you think Trey felt when he found out that his neighbors could overhear conversations on their cordless phone?
- How would you feel if tapes of your phone conversations from this week were played in front of the whole church? Would you be embarrassed by certain things you said?
- How should the Arabies handle this "case of the wandering phone signal"?
- What needs to change about your conversation habits today?

☑ Check It Out

Read James 3:1-12 for a sobering reminder of the power of the tongue, and how we need to use it for good and not for evil.

♡ Apply It

If no human being can control the tongue (James 3:8), why bother trying? Even if we may not achieve perfect control of our tongues, we can still gain enough control to reduce the damage our words can do. It is better to fight a fire than to go around setting new ones. Remember that we are not fighting the tongue's fire in our own strength. The Holy Spirit will give us strength to monitor and control what we say so that whenever our words get off track the Spirit can remind us of God's pattern for our words. Let the Spirit guide and control your speech.

♟ Tip for Parents

One youth leader helped his young people curb gossip with this object lesson. He questioned the truth of the old saying "Sticks and stones may break my bones, but words can never hurt me." He convinced them from their own experiences that words *do* hurt. Then he gave them each a base-ball-sized rock, inscribed (in red nail polish) with "James 3:10." The teens placed these rocks by their telephones as a continual reminder not to say hurtful things over the phone.

Trials

It happened so suddenly. Without warning. Yesterday everything was going smoothly for the Herrens. Today their whole world was turned upside down.

This morning Keith Herren left for work—a middle-level executive's position with a national corporation. He drove his company car out of his nice neighborhood, past the church his family really loves. When he got to the office, he and a number of colleagues were called into the conference room for a surprise meeting. Without warning, the company (like so many others) has decided to downsize for economic reasons. A large number of jobs are being terminated. Keith's is one of those positions.

"Don't worry!" company officials chirped. "There will be a very generous severance package." And it's true that Keith is young enough and talented enough to find another job. But as he drives home he thinks about having to start all over. *Lord, I don't understand. We really love this place. After five moves in ten years, we've finally found a community and a church where we feel at home and where we'd like to put down some roots. And now you're making us start all over again.*

Suddenly Keith's eyes are filled with tears, and he can barely see the road.

◯ Talk about It

- What are some of the trials people are facing in your church?
- What are the big trials your family is having to struggle with?
- Why do you think God allows his children to go through hard times?
- Why do some people seem to go through life and never face any difficulties?
- What would you tell Keith?

☑ Check It Out

Review some of the reasons God may allow hard times in our lives—for instance, to build character (Romans 5:3-4; James 1:3-4) or to demonstrate that our faith is real (1 Peter 1:7).

♡ Apply It

Many people think that believing in God protects them from trouble, so when calamity comes they question God's goodness and justice. But the message of Job is that God allows us to have bad experiences (Job 2:10). Faith in God does not guarantee personal prosperity, and lack of faith does not guarantee trouble. If this were so, people would believe in God simply to get rich and feel better. God is able to rescue us from suffering, but he may also allow suffering to come for reasons we cannot understand. It is Satan's strategy to get us to doubt God at exactly this moment. Job showed a perspective broader than that of seeking his own personal comfort. If we always knew why we were suffering, our faith would have no room to grow.

♟ Tip for Parents

Previous generations seemed to take trials in stride. The current generation seems to be "blown away" by even the slightest difficulties. Why? The answer may lie in the fact that young people today actually expect life to be easy. When it is not (and it rarely is!), they are barely able to cope. We do our kids a great disservice if we lead them to believe that life is going to be gentle and kind to them. If we shelter them from every unpleasant experience, they will never learn to handle trials. Instead, we need to teach them that life is (and will continue to be) difficult. We are fallen creatures in a fallen world. Times will be hard. Paradise will not be ours until heaven. If they can grasp this biblical truth, they will be far ahead of the pack.

Trust

Amy's in a tough spot. Her one remaining kidney is failing. She's had three transplants already. Now it looks like she'll have to go back on dialysis, and back on the list of those awaiting donor organs.

She's scared. She could lose her life.

She's confused. She doesn't understand why God is allowing this to happen.

She's sad. Everything in her life was going really well . . . and now this.

Her parents, meanwhile, are nervously wondering where they are going to find the tens of thousands of dollars they will need to pay for Amy's upcoming medical care.

A whole church is praying, and a whole community is pulling for Amy. Will her story have a happy ending?

○ Talk about It

- Have you ever been in a life-threatening situation? When? What was it like?
- What emotion is the hardest for you to deal with: fear, confusion, sadness, uncertainty, anxiety? Why?
- Where do you turn for comfort when your world falls apart?
- What would you say to someone like Amy?
- What does it mean to you when you hear God and/or Christ referred to as our "shepherd"?

☑ Check It Out

Read Psalm 23, perhaps the most beloved passage in the whole Bible. Listen carefully to what it says about God being our shepherd.

♡ Apply It

In describing the Lord as a shepherd (Psalm 23:1), David wrote out of his own experience because he had spent his early years caring for sheep (1 Samuel 16:10-11). Sheep are completely dependent on the shepherd for provision, guidance, and protection. The New Testament calls Jesus the "good shepherd" (John 10:11); the "great Shepherd" (Hebrews 13:20-21); and the "head Shepherd" (1 Peter 5:4). As the Lord is the good shepherd, so we are his sheep—not frightened, passive animals, but obedient followers, wise enough to follow one who will lead us in the right places and in right ways. Like sheep, we cannot know our shepherd's every purpose. We can only follow him, trusting that he knows the way even if we don't.

▮▮ Tip for Parents

Some years ago, Phillip Keller wrote a wonderfully insightful book entitled *A Shepherd Looks at Psalm 23*. Calling on his own experiences with tending sheep, Keller explains the beautiful imagery of the Twenty-third Psalm. If you have older children or preteens, they will love this book.

Upset

It's a big day for the Oney family. Two weeks ago they purchased their first home! And today—finally—it's moving day.

About twenty friends from church have shown up to help. Parked in the driveway and on the street is a wide assortment of pickup trucks and minivans, some even pulling small trailers. The men are clustered in the kitchen eating doughnuts and drinking coffee. The women are marking boxes and planning what will go where (and when!). Children are whooping and running around in the yard on a picture-perfect day.

About fifteen minutes into the proceedings, Lisa Oney watches in horror as four strong men grab her brand-new refrigerator/freezer, lay it on its side, and then slide it into the back of an old pickup truck containing gravel, rusty tools, and dirt. Lisa winces at the sound of metal rubbing violently over a bumpy surface.

Almost in tears, she pulls her husband, Mark, aside and tells him the story. His heart sinks. "What are we supposed to do?" he mumbles. "How do you say to a bunch of friends, a bunch of supposedly responsible adults, people who are giving up their Saturday to help us, 'Hey! You're tearing up our stuff—cut it out!'?"

"I don't know," Lisa sniffles. "But if we get to the new house and everything's all scratched up and broken, what kind of help is that?"

❂ Talk about It

- What are the ups and downs of moving to a new house? a new city?
- What is your most treasured possession? Why?
- Why don't people seem to care for the things of others as much as they care for their own possessions?
- What are some things Mark and Lisa could do in this awkward situation?
- Talk about a time when someone tried to help you and actually ended up creating a problem.
- How do you think you would respond in a situation like the one above?

✉ Check It Out

Read Ephesians 4:25-27 for a helpful piece of counsel on how to respond to situations like the one faced by the Oneys.

♡ Apply It

The Bible doesn't tell us that we shouldn't feel angry, but it points out that we need to handle our anger properly. If vented thoughtlessly, anger can hurt others and destroy relationships. If bottled up inside, it can cause us to become bitter and destroy us from within. The Bible tells us to deal with our anger immediately in a way that builds relationships rather than destroys them (Ephesians 4:26). If we nurse our anger, we will give Satan an opportunity to divide us. Are you angry with someone right now? What can you do to resolve your differences? Don't let the day end before you begin to work on mending your relationship.

♊ Tip for Parents

Remind your children of the importance of the Golden Rule (i.e., treating others the way you want to be treated—and treating their things the way you want your things to be treated). Perhaps you can even tell about a time in your own life when you broke something that belonged to someone else and you had to own up to (and pay up for) your actions.

Video Games

For his birthday, Dale Dickinson's grandparents got him a new Videotendo Home Entertainment system. Videotendo is the latest, most advanced, most expensive, most awesome video game system available. The graphics and sound are so realistic it's scary!

Dale has been hovering over his new toy all weekend, trying out the different game cartridges he got. He's having a good time, but he's oblivious to the world—a fact which is becoming increasingly irritating to his mom.

After three failed attempts to get Dale's attention, Mrs. Dickinson finally turns to her husband and says, "David, this is really starting to make me mad! It's like he's tuned out everything else. He's a little drone—just sitting there staring at that screen."

"Yeah, well, not only is he wasting a lot of time, but have you seen that one game Aunt Katherine sent?"

"No, which one?"

"I don't know. . . . It's called Gangbuster or something like that. The object of the game is to walk through this city at night and avoid getting killed by these violent gangs."

"Oh, David, that sounds terrible!"

"It is! You should see all the blood and guts."

"I don't want him playing that."

"I'm not sure I want him playing Videotendo at all. It's like he's becoming an addict or something."

⟳ Talk about It

- Why do you think video games are so popular?
- What are the pros and cons of playing video games?
- What guidelines should Christians follow when deciding what video games to play?

☑ Check It Out

The Bible urges God's people to be productive and to avoid wasting time. See 2 Thessalonians 3:6-13.

♡ Apply It

Any sort of overwhelming obsession—whether it be one's work or recreation (in the form of a vehicle, video games, sports, etc.)—is akin to idolatry. When we spend all our time focused on material possessions or pleasures, we waste precious time that could be used for God. The Bible teaches us to "number our days" so that we make the most of the time God has given us. There's a difference between leisure and laziness. Relaxation and recreation provide necessary and much-needed balance to our lives; but when it is time to work, Christians should be ready and willing. We should make the most of our talent and time, doing all we can to provide for ourselves and our dependents. Rest when you should be resting, and work when you should be working.

♟ Tip for Parents

Before correcting your children for "wasting time playing those stupid video games," it might be wise to evaluate your own use of time. Do *you* spend a lot of time watching television or otherwise "wasting" time? Perhaps you can devise a system or schedule for children that permits some playing of video games, but only after other responsibilities have been met. You can keep the game cartridges and let your child check them out, library-style, one at a time.

Violence

You don't realize how many violent images you see in a single day until you stop to add it up. For example, take one day in the life of Stephen.

When he woke up this morning, he watched a few cartoons. In some he saw superheroes beating up the bad guys; in others, Wile E. Coyote trying to kill and eat Road Runner.

In the car on the way to school, he heard a news report on the radio about violent riots in a foreign city.

At school he saw two boys get into a fight at lunchtime over a bag of potato chips.

After school he watched a baseball game on one of the superstations. Suddenly a brawl erupted when one team's pitcher hit a batter on the opposing team. It took the umpires fifteen minutes to restore order.

During the network news, the anchorman reported on the trial of an infamous serial killer.

○ Talk about It

- Why do you think our society is so violent?
- Is violence ever harmless? What about cartoon violence or the violence inherent in sports like football or boxing?
- What, if anything, should parents do to protect their children from seeing or hearing about violent images?
- How do you think Stephen has been or will be affected by the things he observed and heard during the day described above?
- What could be done to make society and individuals less violent?

☑ Check It Out

Note that in Genesis 6:11-13, it was largely because of violence that God decided to judge the world with a flood. See also the warning found in 2 Timothy 3:1-5.

♡ Apply It

Although Noah lived among violent people, he tried to do what pleased God by conducting his affairs according to God's will (Genesis 6:9). For a lifetime he walked step-by-step in faith, a living example to his generation. Like Noah, we live in a world filled with violence. Are we being an influence on others, or are we being influenced? Either the two- or three-foot space around you is becoming more like you or you are becoming more like it. Be a peacemaker.

▮▮ Tip for Parents

If you allow your children to have their own television or videocassette player in their bedrooms, there is no way to monitor what goes into their minds. It's hard to censor even regular television because so many commercials for upcoming shows are filled with rough and lurid images. And the news is generally dominated by stories of violence. One strategy is to get rid of the television and simply have a videocassette player and a monitor. This device can't receive broadcast signals. It can only play videotapes. That way parents *can* carefully control what their children see.

Wasting Time

Last Friday night, Charles spent the night with his friend Arnie Slugbert.

"Hey, how was it?" Charles's mom asked when she picked him up on Saturday. "Did you have fun?"

"Oh, I dunno. It was all right, I guess. We didn't really do much, though."

"What do you mean?"

"I mean we watched TV all night."

"*That* doesn't sound like much fun. I thought you told me Arnie has lots of 'cool stuff.' Didn't you guys want to swim or go fishing in the pond behind his house?"

"Well, *I* did. But Arnie said he was too tired. And so we watched TV. The whole night! Just like we always do at our house. Man, if I just wanted to watch TV, I could have stayed home with you and Dad."

Charles's mom gulped. "Charles, you think that's all we do? Just watch TV? That's not true! We do *lots* of fun things!"

"Like what? Mom, every night from suppertime till bedtime you and Dad just sit in your lounge chairs and watch TV. You don't go anywhere or do anything."

"We go to church!"

"Well, maybe so, but I just feel like the summer is flying by, and before we know it, it's gonna be time to go back to school. And all we're doing is wasting our whole vacation."

○ Talk about It

- What are some of your favorite things to do when you have free time?
- What things (activities, hobbies, responsibilities) tend to take up most of your time?
- If you had an extra six hours a day, what are some things you would like to do?
- What is the difference between relaxing and wasting time?
- Discuss your family's TV-viewing habits. What, if anything, needs to change?
- Is TV viewing a wise use of time? Why or why not?

☑ Check It Out

For a reminder that God wants us to wisely spend our time on earth, see Psalm 90:10-12.

♡ Apply It

Life is short no matter how long we live (Psalm 39:4). If there is something important we want to do, we must not put it off for a better day. Ask yourself, "If I had only six months to live, what would I do?" Would you tell someone that you love him or her? Would you deal with an undisciplined area in your life? Would you tell someone about Jesus? Life is short; don't neglect what is truly important.

♟ Tip for Parents

Television (even if it is free of sex and violence) is detrimental in this sense: It consumes massive amounts of time. And most programming, if you evaluate it objectively, is truly mediocre. You can probably count on one hand the shows you've seen that have had a long-term positive impact on your life. Don't let the "boob tube" consume your family's precious time together! Be creative. Read. Play games. Exercise. Take a walk. Do an experiment. But do *something!* Once your time with your children is gone, it's gone forever!

Wealth

Mark is only twelve, but he has the rest of his life planned out:

"I'm gonna get a scholarship to play basketball at Kentucky. While I'm there, we're gonna win the national championship, and I'm gonna be all-American. Then I'll get drafted and play for the Chicago Bulls and make about five million dollars a year."

That's pretty ambitious, but he's not finished yet. There's more to the plan.

"After I play about ten years, I'll just manage all my money. 'Cause while I'm in college, I'm gonna major in accounting and financial stuff. And I'll keep investing and making more and more money. And finally, when I'm about forty, I'll be set."

Why the obsession with money?

"Things are pretty crazy in this world. My dad says the stock market is unpredictable, and plus you never know if a regular job is going to last. I figure my plan is the best way to be secure."

⟳ Talk about It

- If you could have any job in the world, what would you want to do and why?
- Is it smart to pick a job just on the basis of how much it pays? Why or why not?
- What do you think about Mark's plan? How likely is it to happen?
- Is any kind of wealth (money, savings, possessions, etc.) ever *totally* secure? Why or why not?
- What does it mean to be *spiritually* wealthy?

☑ Check It Out

Before you put too much trust in having money or being wealthy, consider the warning found in Luke 12:19-21.

♡ Apply It

One man's wealth made his life comfortable and gave him power and prestige. When Jesus told him to sell everything he owned, he went away sad (Luke 18:22-23). Jesus was touching the very basis of that man's security and identity. The man did not understand that he would be even more secure if he followed Jesus than he was with all his wealth. Jesus does not ask all believers to sell everything they have, although that may be his will for some. He does ask us all, however, to get rid of anything that has become more important than God. If your basis for security has shifted from God to what you own, it would be better for you to get rid of those possessions.

♟ Tip for Parents

If you're brave enough, ask your children this question: "What would you say Mommy or Daddy trusts in more than anything else?" Depending on how young your kids are, you may want to phrase it in the form of a multiple-choice answer. Give them some options: God, money, a job, friends, prayer, family. Another way to say it is to ask, "What do I talk about or spend time worrying about the most?"

The answer may sting, but it may also show you how you need to change.

Winning and Losing

Because he's three years older, Todd has always been able to beat his sister at any board or card game. For a long time he took advantage of her naïveté: "How about if I give you this pretty purple card called Mediterranean Avenue, and you give me that ugly blue one called Boardwalk?" Later, even after she learned all the rules and the ropes, he simply outsmarted her.

Always Todd reveled in his triumph. Gloating and boasting, he teased Elizabeth to the point of tears.

Today, however, the tide turned. Playing checkers, Elizabeth beat her brother. Actually, the game was never officially completed, for you see, once it became clear to Todd that he was going to lose, he knocked the checkerboard over and tromped out of the room, muttering under his breath.

○ Talk about It

- When you watch a sports event, do you tend to pull for the favored team or person, or do you root for the underdog? Why?
- Do you get upset when you lose? Why or why not?
- Why are some people extremely competitive while others are more laid-back?
- How do you like it when someone beats you at something and then rubs it in?
- Which is worse and why—a person who loses and fusses or a person who wins and gloats?
- What do you think eventually happened between Todd and Elizabeth?

☑ Check It Out

Read about pride—the root cause of our desire to defeat others, as well as our desire to avoid losing—Proverbs 16:5 and 1 Peter 5:5.

♡ Apply It

In Ezekiel's day, the people of Jerusalem took great pride in their buildings. The temple itself was a source of pride (Ezekiel 24:20-21). But God told them that this pride would be crushed when the evil and godless Babylonians destroyed Jerusalem's houses and holy places. If you are going through a humiliating experience, God may be using that experience to weed out pride in your life. Accept it as God's good plan for you.

Tip for Parents

We live in a competitive world, so it's not wise to shield our kids from all forms of competition. Nevertheless, we can minimize the emphasis on competition by playing games "just for the fun of it." Every now and then, refuse to keep score. And if you have a child who acts like Todd, restrict him or her from playing until he or she can exercise some self-control.

Wisdom

Rob seldom pays attention in church, but for some reason, last Sunday was different. The preacher gave a sermon about Solomon, and Rob was truly mesmerized.

What a life! Solomon had incredible wealth, an unbelievable kingdom, more than six hundred wives, and world-famous wisdom. People came from all over just to ask him questions. Solomon always amazed them with his answers.

Lying in a hammock on the back porch that Sunday afternoon, Rob was still thinking about Solomon. *I sure wish I had that much money. Think of all the stuff I could get—any motorcyle I wanted. And if I were wise like that, I'd know what to do about everything: what to say to Katie, how to get away from Terrell, what I should be when I'm older, and how to get Dad to come back.*

○ Talk about It

- What is wisdom, and how is it different from intelligence or knowledge?
- Who is the wisest person you know? Why is he/she so wise?
- How can a person become wise?
- What is the most foolish thing you have ever done?
- Does knowing the Bible make a person wise? Why or why not?
- What are some things you will do this week to increase your wisdom?

☑ Check It Out

Consider what the Bible says is the very source of wisdom—Job 28:28 and Proverbs 9:10.

♡ Apply It

God gave Solomon "a wise and understanding mind" (1 Kings 3:12), but it was up to Solomon to apply that wisdom to all areas of his life. Solomon did use wisdom in governing the nation, but he used foolishness in running his household. Wisdom is both the ability to discern what is best and the strength of character to choose it. While Solomon knew what the wise course of action was, he did not always act upon it (11:6). It's up to you to make wise choices.

♚♚ Tip for Parents

The Hebrew word for wisdom is *hokmah;* it means "skill in living." Wisdom has to do with applied knowledge. It is not enough merely to know what one ought to do. The wise person does what he or she knows is right. Praise your children and affirm them whenever they apply biblical truth to life situations. If you want a Bible that will help you understand how to do that, consult the *Life Application Study Bible.*

Witnessing

Stacy McCullough and Heather Stinson became best friends through school and their involvement in the Girl Scouts. Now the girls are inseparable, and because of their friendship, the families are beginning to spend more time together as well.

The only "problem" with this new development is that Stacy and her parents are Christians, but Heather and her family are not. Most of the time this spiritual difference is insignificant. But every now and then situations arise that highlight the different value systems of the two families. Take last weekend as an example.

The Stinsons called the McCulloughs and invited them to a jazz music festival.

"I've never been to a jazz festival," Sharon McCullough said to her husband as she hung up the phone. "What do you think it's going to be like?"

"Well, I suspect it'll be different. I'm sure there will be a lot of drinking and people dancing and having a good time."

"Do you think we should call the Stinsons back and cancel?"

"Honey, we can't do that! Let's just go and make the most of it."

Well, the weekend came and went. The festival was definitely different. The McCulloughs weren't wild about the music, and some of the Stinsons' other friends were a little bit on the crazy side. But the friendship deepened.

And in the gospel music tent, Helen Stinson leaned over during an old spiritual and whispered to Sharon McCullough, "Do you sing like this at your church? If so, I'd like to come with you sometime."

⟳ Talk about It

- What are the dangers of becoming friends with non-Christians?
- Should Christians do things like go to music festivals with their non-Christian friends? Why or why not?
- What are some ways you could reach out to friends and/or neighbors who do not know Christil?
- Why do so few Christians take the time to develop relationships with lost people?

☑ Check It Out

Read 2 Corinthians 5:17-21 for a good reminder about our mission in the world. Then read John 4:1-42 for an example of dealing with people different from us.

♡ Apply It

As believers, we are Christ's ambassadors, sent with his message of reconciliation to the world. An ambassador of reconciliation has an important responsibility. We dare not take this responsibility lightly. How well are you fulfilling your commission as Christ's ambassador? Jesus spoke with a woman who (1) was a Samaritan, a member of the hated mixed race, (2) was known to be living in sin, and (3) was in a public place. No respectable Jewish man would talk to a woman under such circumstances. But Jesus did. The gospel is for every person, no matter what his or her race, social position, or past sins. We must be prepared to share this gospel at any time and in any place. Jesus crossed all barriers to share the gospel, and we who follow him must do no less.

♊ Tip for Parents

Our kids are excellent evangelistic tools. They easily and naturally form friendships with other children, and through those relationships we can often get to know other parents. Take advantage of these opportunities. Get to know some non-Christians. Then, as Joe Aldrich counsels, "Love them till they ask you why." Then share the love of Christ!

Working Long Hours

Robert and Maureen Fletcher realized a lifelong dream six months ago when they quit their jobs, moved back to their hometown, and started their own computer consulting business.

It's been a real struggle to get the new company up and running. The hours have been long, and the start-up costs high. The Fletcher kids are complaining that they don't ever get to do fun things with Mom and Dad. Even so, Robert and Maureen are enjoying being their own bosses.

"Just a little while longer," Robert keeps saying, "and these eighty-hour weeks will be history. We'll finally be able to get back on a sane schedule. We'll get reacquainted with the kids."

Unfortunately, that day didn't come soon enough. On Tuesday night Robert received an emergency service call forty minutes before his daughter was scheduled to play a part in her school's production of *Our Town.*

"How long will it take?" Maureen asked.

"Probably several hours."

"Can't you go later?" she pleaded as Robert headed out the door.

Robert sighed with a mixture of disappointment and irritation. "If there was any way, you know I would. But this is a big deal! If I can solidify this account, it'll open up all kinds of doors for us."

○ Talk about It

- Kids, how do you feel when your parents have to miss seeing you in a performance or special event?
- Parents, how do you feel when you must miss seeing your child perform?
- If a parent has a job that requires him or her to work long hours week after week, what options does he or she have? What counsel would you give such a person?

☑ Check It Out

How would you apply Psalm 127 to situations like the one above?

♡ Apply It

God is not against human effort. Hard work honors God (Proverbs 31:10-29). But working to the exclusion of rest or to the neglect of family may be a cover-up for an inability to trust God to provide for our needs. We all need adequate rest and times of spiritual refreshment, and Scripture clearly teaches that we are to invest ourselves in our families. Be careful to maintain a balance: Work hard during work time, and honor the times you have set aside for rest, relaxation, and your family.

▮▮ Tip for Parents

If your job requires you to work long hours, sit down with your spouse (or a trusted friend) and brainstorm on some ways you can find more time for family.

Worship

Let's peek in on the various members of Mt. Olive Church as they ride home from church on a sunny Sunday.

Bill Prescott has his window down, and he's singing (at the top of his lungs) a praise chorus they sang in the morning service.

Tori Peterson is wondering why the people at Mt. Olive don't get excited or raise their hands in worship like her church back home does.

Candace Tillsback misses her old church with its candles and big pipe organ and robed choir.

Jessica Wempe is telling a friend that she felt goosebumps at one point in the service. "It was like I could feel the presence of God in that room!"

Mike Veronie is feeling frustrated because he feels so inhibited in Sunday morning worship. "I get so excited at football games, I just about go nuts. Then I get to church, and I sit on my hands because I feel so self-conscious! Why do I get excited over twenty-two guys chasing a ball but not over the God of the universe? What's wrong with me?"

ᗊ Talk about It

- What is worship? How would you define it?
- Why is worship important?
- What's the best worship experience you've ever had? What made it so special?
- Is there a "right" way to worship? Explain.
- When is the best time to worship?
- What do you think about Mike's observation above?
- What could you do today to worship God more effectively?

☑ Check It Out

Read about worship in the psalms (Psalm 100) and in the last book of the Bible (Revelation 5:6-14).

♡ Apply It

Worship involves both celebration and confession (Leviticus 23:23-27). But on Israel's national holidays, the balance was heavily tipped in favor of celebration—five joyous occasions to two solemn occasions. The God of the Bible encourages joy! God did not intend for us only to meditate and introspect. He also wants us to celebrate. Serious reflection and immediate confession of sin is essential. But this should be balanced by celebrating who God is and what he has done for his people.

ᝫᝫ Tip for Parents

Our word *worship* comes from an old English word *worthship,* and it conveys the idea of declaring the value or worth of something. To worship God means we declare that he is precious and valuable to us. The question is not "Will we worship?" We will. By our very nature we are worshiping creatures. The question is *"Who* or *what* will we worship?" Whatever or whomever we devote our time, energy, effort, and resources to, *that* is what we value, and, therefore, what we worship.